PEARSON CUSTOM

STUDENT SUCCESS & CAREER DEVELOPMENT

Liberal Arts Humanities
Introductory Seminar   LAH 100
Dutchess Community College

Pearson Learning Solutions

New York   Boston   San Francisco
London   Toronto   Sydney   Tokyo   Singapore   Madrid
Mexico City   Munich   Paris   Cape Town   Hong Kong   Montreal

Senior Vice President, Editorial and Marketing: Patrick F. Boles
Sponsoring Editor: Debbie Coniglio
Operations Manager: Eric M. Kenney
Marketing Manager: Kathleen Kourian
Production Manager: Jennifer Berry
Database Project Specialist: Sean Pantellere
Cover Designer: Kristen Kiley

Published in the United States of America.

Please visit our web site at *www.pearsoncustom.com*

Attention bookstores: For permission to return unused stock, call 800-777-6872.

Pearson Learning Solutions, 501 Boylston Street, Suite 900, Boston, MA 02116
A Pearson Education Company
www.pearsoned.com

ISBN 10: 0-558-61475-2
ISBN 13: 978-0-558-61475-1

Contents

Understanding College Culture and Your Campus

1

Understanding College Culture and Your Campus

Four Student Stories: Orientation

Passports, disposable cameras, and plastic leis are scattered all over the tables; fake palm trees rustle from the movement underneath them; and the smell of coconut fills the air in the student center. "Destination: Degree," the travel-themed orientation, is winding down after an afternoon of skits, presentations, and door prizes of pink flamingo keychains and T-shirts.

"If everyone will score their inventories, we will explain how learning style preference affects your study habits," says Jason, an orientation leader who is wearing an orange "Ask me!" T-shirt and a camera around his neck.

Dozens of students are gathered next to tables where student leaders and counselors hand out T-shirts, water bottles, and welcome packets.

"Hey, I am 'kinesthetic,' which means I learn best by using body movements. That kind of makes sense. I teach kickboxing and learned how to do it by working out almost every day," Evan tells the group.

"I thought I would be more of a social learner, but my learning style preference is individual," says Michael as he rubs his head. "I spent so much time leading troops when I was in the military."

"I am definitely 'aural,'" Laura says to the group. "I got through all my classes in high school by listening to the lectures. I rarely took notes because I liked to listen."

"Yeah, I can see that. You talked during every presentation!" Evan jokes.

Juanita, the youngest of the group, twists her mouth and wrinkles her forehead. "Will you be able to do that in college, just listen?" she asks. "I mean, I have heard that the professors expect so much more of you when it comes to being in class. Seems like there is more to do than just listen."

"I am sure you will," says Michael. "My girlfriend graduated last year with a degree in nursing, and it seems like all she did was read for class and then study her notes every night."

"Yeah, that makes sense. If anyone needs someone to study with, let me know. I am an early morning person. I took dual enrollment classes in high school and did best in my earliest classes," Juanita says.

Evan, who has been looking over his orientation information, looks up when he hears Juanita's offer. "If you want to learn a few kickboxing moves in exchange for help taking notes, let me know," Evan says to Juanita.

"Sounds good!" Juanita laughs.

With neon green note cards in her hand, Jasmine approaches the group's table. She passes cards to Laura, Michael, Evan, and Juanita. "Take these cards," Jason says, "and write down what you think will be your biggest challenge in college."

"If anyone wants to exchange a home-cooked meal for some babysitting while I study, let me know, too," says Laura, continuing the conversation. "Balancing family, a job, and college full-time," she prints on the card.

Michael writes his down: "Worried I am too old to go back to school. Can't teach an old dog new tricks." Juanita writes, "Not sure what degree or career I want," and Evan records, "Meeting new people."

As the four of them hand in their cards, they gather their backpacks and the college planners they received when they signed in for orientation.

Michael gives the group his number before they leave. "I know Laura is the talkative one, but give me a call if you ever need anything. Good luck to everyone!" he says.

In This Chapter

Evan, Laura, Michael, and Juanita will soon discover the expectations of college, and after participating in orientation, they should be well prepared to handle the changes they may encounter from their previous roles and routines: Evan has worked full-time for the past two years; Laura has been a stay-at-home mother; Michael has been in the military; and Juanita has just graduated from high school. Just as these four students have been oriented to college life, the purpose of this chapter is to introduce you to this new culture, to reveal the truths about higher education, to debunk the myths, and to prepare you for meeting the challenges that you will inevitably face. This chapter also provides you with information about what this new environment will look like and what you can expect in terms of communication between the college and you.

More specifically, at the end of this chapter you will be able to do the following:

* Describe what college will be like and what the expectations are.

* Explain the differences between high school/work and college.

* Identify key campus features and information.

What Is College Culture?

Every day, we are bombarded by offers to get something without effort and without sacrificing our precious time. We have come to value anything that is quick and easy. Unfortunately, the desire for "quick and easy" has spread from fast food and convenience items to higher education as well. Students who are strapped for time but who believe that a degree will give them the financial stability and career success they want often enroll in a community college because the programs are typically shorter than those at a four-year university—the "quick" that some students are seeking. Other students enroll in a community college because they believe that the courses are not as challenging as they would be at other schools—the "easy" those students are seeking.

The degree programs at community colleges are shorter, usually requiring one or two years, but the reality is that you may need to take more time to complete a degree program if you plan to enroll as a part-time student. Also, if you need developmental or remedial classes before you can start on the required curriculum, completion of the program will be delayed.

Community college classes and degree programs are as demanding as their equivalents at four-year universities. Because of technical and industrial standards and career licensing, many courses and programs are, in fact, very challenging. Instructors who teach in the technical, industrial, and business fields are expected to graduate students who can pass licensing exams, which means the standards in the class must be high. If the courses were "easy," then the graduates would be unemployable. Likewise, students who intend to transfer to four-year universities after they complete their general education requirements would not be successful after transfer if the courses they took at the community college were not challenging. Community colleges want well-prepared and successful graduates; thus, it is in their best interest to provide courses that require the best work from their students.

Making the Transition

High School to College or Work to College

For some students, the move from high school to college seems fairly simple—both require reading, writing, testing, and attending class. Students who are taking the step from work to school may also see some similarities between their jobs and their classroom work—both require working hard, keeping yourself motivated, and following the rules. If the differences between high school or work and college are that similar, then why do so many college students have difficulty making a successful transition?

The answer to that question can be given by the instructors who see smart, competent students have trouble adjusting to the climate and culture of college because they do not understand what is expected of them. In other words, in order to be successful, students must know what is expected of them beyond the questions on the next test; they need to know how college works and how to navigate through not only their courses, but also the common challenges that they will face as they work toward a degree or certificate.

Table 1 illustrates some of the differences and similarities among high school, a full-time job, and college. Notice that the greatest differences occur between high

TABLE 1   Differences Among High School, Full-Time Work, and College

High School	Full-Time Work	College
Attendance is mandatory in order to meet requirements	Attendance is mandatory in order to stay employed	Attendance may not be mandatory
At least 6 continuous hours spent in class each day	At least 8 continuous hours spent at work each day	Different amounts of time spent in class and between classes each day
Very little choice in what classes you take and when you take them	May have little choice in work assignments and when the work is to be completed	More flexibility in when you work on assignments and how soon you complete them before the due date
Moderate to no outside work necessary to be successful	Moderate to no overtime work necessary to complete job duties	Substantial amount of outside work to complete assignments and to be successful
Teachers check homework and keep you up-to-date on progress; they will inform you if you are not completing assignments and progressing well	Supervisors check completion and quality of work at regular intervals; they will inform you if you are not meeting the standards for the position	Professors may not check all homework or provide feedback on progress at regular intervals; they may not inform you if you are not meeting the standards of the course
Teachers go over material and expect you to remember facts and information	Employers provide basic information, expect you to use it to complete the job effectively	Professors provide concepts and theories and expect you to evaluate the ideas, synthesize the ideas with other concepts you have learned, and develop new theories
Frequent tests over small amounts of material allow for grades to be raised if needed	Supervisors create employee improvement plans to allow you to improve your ratings if needed	Professors provide the standards and grading criteria but often allow only a few chances (through infrequent testing/assignments) to meet them

school and college. There are some similarities between a full-time job and college, although there are also distinct differences.

Go for the Gold by Remembering S.I.L.V.E.R.

Making a successful transition will not only include comparing where you have just come from (home, work, or another institution of learning) to college life, but it will also involve breaking down the experience into parts that you can master. To remember what you need to start and end well, remember this simple acronym: **S.I.L.V.E.R.** This stands for Supplies, Instructors' Expectations, Learning, Vocabulary, Effort, and Responsibility.

Supplies, or "The Right Stuff." Making sure you are adequately prepared for the journey you are about to take is the first step in being successful. You wouldn't head out on a trip to unknown lands without a map, proper gear, and plenty of food and water! Think of your college supplies as part of your survival gear, too. The most important items that you will need at the beginning of the semester are required textbooks and course materials. You can find out what books and materials you will need either through the bookstore or through your professors. Usually an exact list of course materials is included in your syllabus. In high school books and course materials are provided for each student, but in college, you will be responsible for obtaining and purchasing your own materials—and you will need to do that before or at the very beginning of the semester. Trying to get by without the textbook or required calculator or software can seriously hurt your chances of success and is not recommended. If you find yourself unable to acquire or buy your materials, then you will need to talk to your instructor immediately to ask about alternative arrangements.

In addition to books and materials, you may also need access to a computer. Your professors will expect that you have a working knowledge of how to use one. If you do not have the skills needed to use a computer, then seek help from computer lab technicians, special computer classes, and classmates. Most colleges provide computer labs, email accounts, and printers for student use, but their hours may be limited; they may be crowded at busy times during the semester; and you may have to pay for the pages that you print. Thus, having the necessary computer skills as well as regular access to a computer will be integral to your success, and if you need some help honing those skills, your college may offer computer classes.

Other "right stuff" items include paper (for both note-taking and printing purposes), pens, a dictionary, a writing handbook, and a thesaurus. As you take more classes, you may need specialized reference books and supplies, such as a specialized calculator, to help you study and complete assignments. A good, sturdy backpack that allows you to carry all the books and notebooks will also be essential. Since you will not have a locker or place to store your things between classes, you will have to find a bag that holds up to the task of carrying heavy materials over a period of weeks. One other item that new students need, which is becoming more essential each year, is a portable storage device that will hold your computer files and allow you to access them at any computer. Thumb drives, also known as flash drives and pin drives, are increasingly popular because they hold a large amount of files and because they are easy to carry.

Instructors' Expectations. In addition to your supplies, knowing and meeting your instructors' expectations will make a great foundation for success. One essential expectation that instructors have is preparation—yours. You should be prepared *before* you get to class by reading the assigned pages or completing the homework. Instructors who assign reading or homework expect students to prepare—they may even administer quizzes to ensure that students have prepared—and to ask questions about anything they did not understand. Instructors may assume that if you don't ask questions or participate in a discussion, you understand the assignment. They may also hold you accountable for the assigned reading on exams even though it was not discussed in class.

Another expectation is that out-of-class assignments must be typed; in fact, unless otherwise stated, assume that all outside assignments should be word-processed, because they are easier to read and they look more professional. If you don't know how to use a word processor, now is the time to learn; relying on others to word-process your work could put you at a disadvantage. You may not be able to control when the person can complete the work, which can make you miss assignment due dates.

Instructors also expect that college students are able to access technology regularly and use it competently. What this means is that your professor will assume and expect that you have consistent access to a computer and the Internet. She will also believe that you have an email account and can send emails—even messages with attachments—successfully. If these are skills and equipment that you do not have, you will need to find out where you can access a computer on campus or off campus and make sure that you have the ability to use it properly.

One last expectation—but not the only one left—is that instructors expect you to use their office hours, the time they are scheduled to be in their offices, to meet with them if you have any questions or need anything. This is a time not only to address any concerns you may have about your progress, but it is also a wonderful time to get to know your professors better.

Collaboration

Working with a group, create a list of 10 expectations of your instructors that you have discovered so far this semester. Divide your list into expectations that you feel you can meet and those that may be challenging for you.

EXERCISE 1

Learning. Taking responsibility for your learning is the cornerstone for college success, and in college you will be actively involved in the learning process. Being an *active* learner means that you are no longer a passive participant in your education, listening to a lecture or reading recreationally. Instead, college classes require that you participate in your own learning by reading actively and critically, by listening actively and critically, by completing assignments, by working with other students, and by making connections among the courses you are taking and your life. Active learners also seek out more information about topics and look for ways to improve their understanding of concepts by seeking help when needed. In essence, active learners make their education a top priority.

One of the most important shifts in thinking about your learning experience in college is the various ways and places that learning and student support can take place outside the classroom. Eventually, Michael will face his fear of asking for help by seeking help in the tutoring center, and as he discovers, the classroom is not the only place meaningful learning experience happens! Professors routinely direct students to learning labs, tutors, or supplemental instruction to help students bolster the learning that takes place in the classroom. Consider, then, that classroom learning is only a fraction of the time and activity that you will experience. In fact, if you follow the

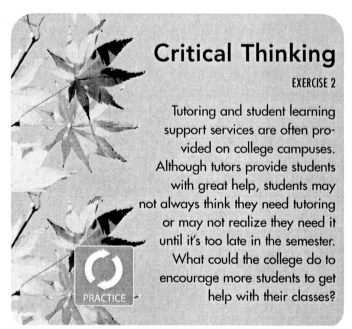

Critical Thinking

EXERCISE 2

Tutoring and student learning support services are often provided on college campuses. Although tutors provide students with great help, students may not always think they need tutoring or may not realize they need it until it's too late in the semester. What could the college do to encourage more students to get help with their classes?

PRACTICE

model of how many hours you are in class a week and how many hours a week you should spend studying, class time is only one-fourth of the time you should be spending learning. The rest of that time, of course, will be spent preparing for class, but it can also be spent working one-on-one with a tutor or reviewing notes and studying with a group. That means that 75% of your time should be spent on activities that contribute to your learning when you are in class.

Vocabulary. With a new environment comes a new language. It won't be too long before you are talking about an AA, GPA, and FERPA all at one time. Knowing what terms mean when they are used will make communication clearer. For example, do you know what a credit hour is? It is the unit of measurement that colleges use that usually equals the amount of time you are in class each week during a 16-week semester. What about FERPA? This initialism stands for Family Educational Rights and Privacy Act, and it is important to know because it determines who can access and discuss your grades or other official records. In college, if you are age 18 and over, only you

TABLE 2   Common College Terms

Term	Definition
AA	Associate of Arts; a degree program that community colleges offer that consists of about 60 credit hours; usually transfers to a four-year institution as part of the core curriculum
AAS	Associate of Applied Science; a degree program that community colleges offer that consists of about 60 credit hours; usually does not contain as many core courses as an AA and is not intended for transfer, but is intended for students who will enter the workforce after graduation
Academic integrity	Doing honest work on all assignments and tests
AS	Associate of Science; a degree program that community colleges offer that consists of about 60 credit hours; usually transfers to a four-year institution as part of the core curriculum; emphasizes science courses
Core curriculum	Also called general education requirements or basic courses; the common courses that almost all students who earn a bachelor's degree complete
Credit hour	The unit of measurement that colleges use that usually equals the amount of time you are in class each week during a 16-week semester
Degree plan	A list of classes that you must complete successful in order to be awarded a degree
FAFSA	Free Application for Federal Student Aid; a form that is completed each year to determine financial aid eligibility
FERPA	Family Educational Rights and Privacy Act; Federal law that regulates the communication and dissemination of your educational records
GPA	Grade Point Average; each grade that is earned is awarded grade points that are multiplied by the number of credit hours taken; the result is the grade point average

will be the one who discusses your grades with your professor. If others, such as a spouse, parent, or employer, wants to know how you are doing, then you can allow them access to that information by letting a college official know. Table 2 provides just a handful of the vocabulary that you will learn in college.

Effort. Woody Allen once said, "Eighty percent of success is showing up." Definitely, in college classes, you can't be successful unless you attend regularly. College professors may not take attendance or may not make an issue of students who do not attend; however, it is still your responsibility to attend. If you are receiving financial aid through grants or loans, your attendance may be important to your continuing to receive funds in the future. Some colleges require students to pay back funds received if they fail to attend classes regularly.

Irregular attendance will not only mean missed lectures and jeopardized financial aid, but also mean missed information about assignments, tests, and grading. Especially in courses that build on concepts (such as math, foreign languages, and writing), your lack of attendance can lead to problems with successfully doing assignments and performing on tests later in the semester.

Students who are well prepared for class improve their chances of success.

Peter Finger/PH College

If you miss a class or intend to miss a class, you should mention this to your professor. Although you may not need a doctor's excuse, you should be prepared to justify your absence, especially if you have missed an exam. Most professors, though, may not care why you were absent or may not distinguish between excused or unexcused absences. Instead, they may be more interested that you do not miss very many classes and that you keep up with the work.

Attending class is just part of the effort you will put forth; you will also need to produce quality work. Writing a paper and turning it in is only part of the requirement. You also have to adhere to the standards of the course. If your professor asks for a 10-page paper that argues a contemporary topic and uses five sources, you must follow those guidelines. In some instances, you may receive no credit for completing an assignment if you have not followed these requirements.

The more time you work to complete an assignment *usually* translates to better quality, but this is not always the case. For example, someone who types 30 words a minute will need less time to produce the same typographical-error-free assignments as someone who "hunts and pecks" at the keyboard. The quality of your work is what you will be graded on, not the number of hours you spend doing it.

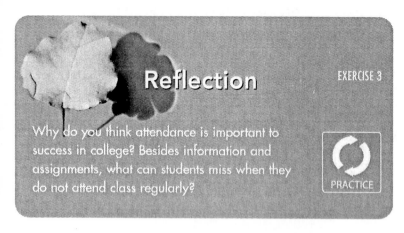

Reflection   EXERCISE 3

Why do you think attendance is important to success in college? Besides information and assignments, what can students miss when they do not attend class regularly?

PRACTICE

Responsibility. No doubt you already juggle numerous responsibilities, and going to class and studying are just more tasks that you must complete each week. Handling your responsibilities skillfully will take a positive attitude, respect for yourself, and maturity. Laura knows how important being responsible for herself and her son is. She has had many years of relying on herself and a few family members to meet her responsibilities. Obviously, as a student she has the responsibility to take notes, study for tests, and attend classes regularly. But she also has the responsibility to ask questions when she doesn't understand or to resolve any conflict that may occur.

With responsibility also comes maturity, which is the foundation for many of the other components of college culture. Without a mature attitude and outlook, the other parts are unattainable. There are, however, less obvious actions that can help you present yourself as a dedicated, mature student. The first one is paying attention during lectures, presentations, talks by guest speakers, and videos. Although this sounds obvious, it is sometimes forgotten after the first few weeks of the semester. For now, work on looking at the front of the room and avoiding distractions. A common barrier to paying attention, besides staring out the window, is doing homework in class. Instructors frown on students who use class time to study for other classes or complete assignments that were due at the beginning of class. Just remember that the instructor sees what you are doing—that you are not paying attention—and will make note of it.

Small actions, but equally important ones, that convey maturity and readiness to meet college expectations include staying for the duration of the class, limiting off-topic conversations with classmates, refraining from eating or participating in distracting activities, and getting ready to exit class only after the instructor has dismissed everyone. One small activity that causes big problems in class is the use of cell phones, headsets, and other electronic communication devices. In some classes, such as a chemistry lab, the distraction can be dangerous. Some colleges have strict policies forbidding the use of cell phones and pagers in class. There may be exceptions, however. For example, if you work in a field that requires your immediate attention in the event of an emergency or if you have a gravely ill family member, ask if you may leave these electronic devices turned on. If your college does not have a policy, turn off your cell phone and pager in class anyway. Students who answer social calls in class appear immature and unconcerned about their education.

A more important way to demonstrate maturity in college is to understand and appreciate constructive criticism from your instructor. When you receive advice or comments about your work or progress in the course, look at it as an opportunity to learn more about yourself and the expectations of college. The instructor's job is to educate you and help you learn more about the world; it is not the instructor's job to undermine those efforts by cutting you down.

Although it is a great confidence builder, positive feedback does not necessarily challenge you to do better or indicate where you can improve. Be open to the challenge of receiving constructive criticism about the quality of your work. It takes a mature person to value constructive criticism and learn from it and a mature person to remember that your professors, counselors, and advisors want to help you be successful, so they will often set high standards that they know you can achieve.

It is worth mentioning here that dealing with diversity, conflict, and controversy takes a certain level of maturity. Effectively meeting any challenge to your belief system or values will demand that you act with integrity and openness. Because the purpose of getting an education is to stretch your mind and expand your ideas, you will need maturity to help you put all that new information into perspective.

The Nitty-Gritty of College

Now you know what to expect and what is expected of you in college, but understanding a few other customary practices will help you go from being a "tourist" to a "native." In other words, the following information will provide you with a better understanding of how college works beyond what happens in the classroom.

Schedules

First, it is helpful to note that colleges organize class time around semesters or terms, which can be as short as 4 weeks, usually during the summer, or as long as 16 weeks. Many colleges have at least four semesters: fall, spring, first summer term and second summer term; the summer terms are shorter than the fall and spring terms. Other colleges organize the academic calendar around 10- or 11-week terms. If you are unsure how many weeks the semester is, count the number of weeks from the first day of class until the last day of finals. You can find the information in the college catalog or in the course outline of your syllabus.

No matter how many weeks you spend taking a course, each semester classes are scheduled at different days during the week. This arrangement may differ significantly from your high school schedule. In college, you may take classes once a week, as is the case in evening or night classes, or you may take them on Mondays, Wednesdays, and Fridays or just Tuesdays and Thursdays. Usually, colleges do not offer classes on Friday nights, so if you take classes in the evening, you will take them either once a week or twice a week, Mondays through Thursdays.

Exceptions to this schedule occur during shortened terms such as summer semesters or intercession terms in which you may go every day during the week. Also, you may have a lab or special class that meets only once a week, but is tied to another class such as biology or chemistry. The best advice for new students is to read the schedule of classes carefully before registering, and as always, ask an advisor, counselor, instructor, or fellow student if you have trouble reading your schedule.

Colleges award credit hours (remember this term from earlier in the chapter?) based on how many hours a week you are in class during a regular semester (summer or intercession terms will double or quadruple the number of hours a week as compared to a regular semester). Thus, a three-credit hour class will require that you spend about three hours in class per week—some classes may last only 50 minutes three times a week. Exceptions do exist: Labs are often worth one credit hour, but they may meet for more than one hour one day a week.

Exhibit 1 shows a typical schedule of a full-time student. Notice the "TR" under the "Days" column; "T" stands for Tuesday and "R" stands for Thursday. Thus, the biology class meets both Tuesday and Thursday while the lab meets on Thursday only. Labs and other special classes may meet for more than one hour a

EXHIBIT 1   16-week class schedule

FALL 2010 (16-WEEK) SCHEDULE

COURSE ID	COURSE NAME	DAYS	TIME	CREDIT HOURS
ENGL 030	COMPOSITION FUNDAMENTALS	MWF	8:00–8:50 a.m.	3.0
BIOL 110	BIOLOGY	TR	8:00–9:15 a.m.	3.0
BIOL 112	BIOLOGY LAB	R	9:25–11:25 a.m.	1.0
MATH 034	INTERMEDIATE ALGEBRA	MWF	10:00–10:50 a.m.	3.0
COLL 101	FRESHMAN SEMINAR	TR	12:15–1:30 p.m.	3.0
TOTAL HOURS				13.0

week, but they are usually worth only one credit hour. Although the classes in this schedule meet two and a half hours each week, they are given three credit hours. Three hours is often an approximation of the time spent in class.

If the schedule in Exhibit 1 reflects a 16-week semester, this student will spend over 40 hours in class for the semester. During summer or intercession terms, you will spend about the same number of hours in class, but you will attend class more often and for a longer period of time.

Because Exhibit 2 is a schedule for a four-week term, the classes meet for more than three hours a week. In this case, students meet for 10 hours a week for 4 weeks, which will equal 40 hours or the equivalent of the total number of hours a 3-credit-hour class will meet during a 16-week term.

Controversial Content

For the most part, college will be a straightforward experience—you will learn the expectations and when you meet them, you will be successful. There are, though, other aspects of college culture that may be uncomfortable or even shocking to you. As stated above, all colleges value diversity, whether it is in the student body population or in the

EXHIBIT 2   4-week class schedule

SUMMER 2011 (4-WEEK) CLASS SCHEDULE

COURSE ID	COURSE NAME	DAYS	TIME	CREDIT HOURS
MATH 101	COLLEGE ALGEBRA	MTWRF	8:00–10:00 a.m.	3.0
ENGL 101	COMPOSITION I	MTWRF	10:10–12:10 p.m.	3.0
TOTAL				6.0

backgrounds of its faculty. Most definitely, you will find diversity in ideas and theories among the subjects that are offered. Some of these ideas and theories may challenge your beliefs and values. Still other subjects may contain material that you find disrespectful, offensive, distasteful, or disturbing. Besides the reading and discussing of controversial or uncomfortable issues, your college may produce student and faculty work that contains language, images, or situations that you find offensive.

What should you do if you encounter college "culture shock"? First, remember that the purpose of higher education is to provide you with a wider worldview and understanding of diversity—even if that diversity involves different ideas, theories, and methods of representing those ideas and theories. Second, remember that you have the right to an opinion and a feeling about what you encounter in college. There is no reason you should hide your feelings or attitudes about what you are learning and encountering. With this said, the third point to remember is that with your right to an opinion, you also have an obligation as a college student to examine your previously held beliefs and evaluate how they are being challenged in your courses or as you participate in college activities. You also have the obligation to appreciate that there is more than one way to view an "offensive" idea or image. Exhibit 3 provides a list of possible subjects that could be controversial to you or other students.

Grades

What is a discussion about college expectations without mentioning grades? For sure, grades are an important part of your education, and at the same time they are unimportant. How can something be both important and unimportant? Grades are important because they often reflect your level of achievement on an assignment or in a course; they are also important for obtaining and maintaining scholarships and financial aid. Additionally, grades are important to family, friends, and employers who may

---

EXHIBIT 3   A sample of possible controversial subjects

The existence of God, higher being

Conservatism and liberalism

Nudity in art, photography

Sexuality, including homosexuality and adultery

The creation of the universe

The theory of extraterrestrial life

Evolution

The beginning of life

Scientific investigation and experimentation (stem cells, cloning)

Socioeconomic theory

be supporting you financially and emotionally. Many people view grades as a reflection of a level of success. For instance, most of the people you ask would view a student who has straight A's as someone who is smart and successful. Earning good grades can motivate you to do your best and give you more confidence as you earn them.

Although good grades feel great when you earn them, grades are not always an indication of your success or lack of success in mastering a subject. James M. Banner, Jr. and Harold C. Cannon (1999), in their book *The Elements of Learning,* define grades as the following: "Grades are evaluations of your work, not of your character or intelligence. You may be a wonderful person but a failure as a biologist. You may find it impossible to do satisfactory work in history but may excel in all other subjects" (p. 160). Banner and Cannon assert, therefore, that grades have limitations. They are a necessary part of evaluation, much as you are evaluated on your job. However, as Banner and Cannon point out, grades do not show the whole picture of who you are. Grades, then, are only part of the story of your education.

If grades only sometimes indicate a level of success in a course and sometimes not, what are you to do? How will you know when to worry about your grades and when to concentrate on learning the material? The purpose of this chapter is to help you answer these questions for yourself by explaining how professors grade and how you can make good grades in college. The chapter also discusses what you can do to de-emphasize making a good grade and increase your attention on mastering the material of the course. This is not to say, however, that grades are never important. They are important because they are a way to describe the work you have done in a class. However, grades alone are not the magic carpet to success in college; they are only part of the story of your achievements. Your goal should be to strike a balance between caring about your grades and caring about improving your skills and increasing your knowledge.

As stated earlier, college professors grade a student on his or her ability to meet the standards of the course or of a particular assignment. Effort is definitely a necessary part of earning good grades—and you will earn the respect of your professor and fellow students by demonstrating an intense effort to master the concepts of a class—but it is only one part of achieving success in a course. College professors expect that you also meet the standards, sometimes called grading criteria, of the course. Exhibit 4 shows a potential set of criteria for a college-level paper. In this case, the criteria are for an A paper.

EXHIBIT 4   Grading criteria for an A paper

- An excellent introduction with engaging hooks, setup, plan for essay, and/or main idea

- An original, significant thesis that offers insightful interpretation or thought

- An inventive and logical organizational plan

- Smooth and varied transitional expressions, phrases, and sentences that provide unity and coherence

- Strong conclusion that ends the essay effectively

- Expressive, clear style with sophisticated sentence structure and word choice

- No more than three major grammatical errors

Knowing how your college assesses student performance is a start to improving your overall outlook on grading. The following is a typical grading scale in college:

90–100 A
80–89   B
70–79   C
60–69   D
50–59   F

Some colleges may use a + or − next to a letter grade such as A− or C+. Usually, colleges that allow for +'s and −'s will also alter the grading scale to designate the different grades. Here is an example of a grading scale that includes +'s and −'s:

94–100 A
90–93   A−
87–89   B+
84–86   B
83–80   B−

Each semester, the registrar will calculate your grade point average, or GPA, and post it to your transcript. Because the calculation of your GPA requires a little mathematical skill, it is important to know how your registrar figures it. Hours are the number of hours you are in class each week. As discussed above, classes are usually three-credit hours. Science or specialized classes that have labs usually carry four-credit hours. Depending on the course and the program, credit hours can be as many as six or as few as one. To know how many hours a course carries, check the description in the college catalog, because some classes meet for more hours a week than they are worth in terms of credit.

Letter grades carry a point value called quality points. Exhibit 5 shows how many quality points each letter grade is worth.

Courses that are designated developmental or remedial usually do not figure into your grade point average, so they do not carry any quality points. If you audit a course or receive AP or CLEP credit for a course, you will not receive quality points either. In other words, while you receive credit on your transcript for taking the course or taking an equivalent of the course, the course will not factor into your

EXHIBIT 5   Grades and quality points

LETTER GRADE	QUALITY POINTS
A	4
B	3
C	2
D	1
F	0

EXHIBIT 6   GPA calculation table

HOURS	GRADE (QUALITY POINTS)	HOURS × GRADE (QUALITY POINTS)
3	A (4)	3 × 4 = 12
3	B (3)	3 × 3 = 9
3	C (2)	3 × 2 = 6
3	C (2)	3 × 2 = 6
3	C (2)	3 × 2 = 6
15 Hours		39 Grade Points

grade point average. Before you figure your GPA, you will need to figure your grade points for each class. You arrive at your grade points by multiplying the quality points for the grade you received by the number of hours the class is worth. For instance, if you took a four-hour class and you made a B, then you will multiply 4 (hours) by 3 (quality points for a B).

Evan is taking 15 hours (5 three-hour courses) this semester; if he receives an A, B, and three C's, then his grade would be calculated as shown in Exhibit 6. Finally, divide the grade points total by the hours total (39/15). Evan's GPA would be 2.6.

What Does Your College Look Like?

Now that you have a better understanding of college culture and what is expected of you, it is time to examine how your college looks. Getting to know the layout of the campus and the people who work there is important to understanding the culture. For example, knowing where to go when you need to use a computer will make your ability to complete an assignment a little easier. Finding your professor's office may save you time and stress when you need to talk to him about an upcoming test. Of course, the more you are on campus, the better able you will be to find people and places that will help you no matter what you need.

The Campus

Find a map of your campus and study it for a few minutes. How many buildings does it have? How much parking space? How much "green" space or landscaping? Are there any unique features to your campus that make it an inviting and exciting place? Familiarizing yourself with your campus is probably the first activity you did when you enrolled in classes. If you have not taken a tour or simply walked around the campus, do so within the first few weeks of the semester. Locate the library, the student center, student parking, the bookstore, the business office, and the registrar's office—just to name a few destinations.

TABLE 3 Campus Layout Checklist

Building or Area	At My College	Not Sure
Student center or union		
Library		
Bookstore		
Administration building		
Theater or auditorium		
Snack bar or food court		
Athletic training facilities (indoor or outdoor)		
Science labs		
Technical and industrial training facilities		
Computer labs		
Separate divisions (such as technical and industrial, computer information systems, allied health, business, general education)		
Individual departments (such as accounting, drafting, welding, natural sciences)		
Student parking		
Benches and tables for meeting outside		
Quiet study space inside		

The more you know about your campus's layout, the easier it will be to find what you are looking for when you need it most. Using your map of the campus or your memory, check off in Table 3 the types of buildings or departments within buildings that you know are present at your college.

If your college has more than one campus, familiarize yourself with the layout of other college property. You may have to travel to a satellite campus to take a test or to pick up materials for a class. If you have the time and the other campus is not too far away, ask for a tour. At the very least, familiarize yourself with any of the items you marked "not sure" in Table 3.

College Publications

Knowing where to go to find services and people is only part of learning about your college. Another important aspect is finding and using the information that the college produces for students. College publications are a great place to find information about courses, programs, scholarships, activities, and policy changes. It is important that you regularly read these publications in order to stay up-to-date with what is going on.

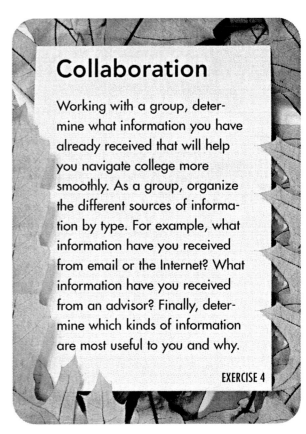

Collaboration

Working with a group, determine what information you have already received that will help you navigate college more smoothly. As a group, organize the different sources of information by type. For example, what information have you received from email or the Internet? What information have you received from an advisor? Finally, determine which kinds of information are most useful to you and why.

EXERCISE 4

College Catalog

The college catalog is an essential document during your academic career. All the information that you need to apply for financial aid, to choose courses, and to graduate is contained in the catalog. You will also find out what you are required to do to complete a degree. The academic calendar is usually placed at the beginning of the catalog. There you will find the dates for registering, dropping courses, and taking final exams.

It is important to read and keep your college catalog because if the college changes any requirements of your degree program, you will be able to follow the guidelines that were published the year you began the program. For instance, if you are working on an office management degree and you have taken three semesters of courses so far, you will not necessarily have to adhere to new requirements that are made at a later date.

Student Handbook

The student handbook, which provides you with specific information about student conduct, academic standards, and services, is another valuable publication. Usually, the handbook contains descriptions of career services, the bookstore, computer labs, and financial aid offices. Academic information including probation and suspension for misconduct and qualifications for making the dean's list can also be found in the student handbook. Most schools view the student handbook as a legal document that outlines what students can do in certain situations, so be sure to read it closely and keep a copy at home or in your book bag.

Campus Safety Brochure

A smaller, but no less important, document that your college publishes is the campus safety and security brochure; in some cases, your college may publish this information on the website instead of printing the material. Whatever the form, this information can include policies on handling sexual assault, substance and drug abuse, and harassment. Also, you can find contact numbers for campus police as well as crime statistics for the campus.

College Newspaper

College newspapers differ from the college catalog and student handbook in that students are usually the ones who are responsible for the content. Within a college

INTEGRITY MATTERS

The student handbook usually contains the college's academic integrity policy, a policy that covers any act that shortcuts the learning process and calls into question a student's integrity as it relates to academic matters. If you are not familiar with academic integrity policies, be sure to read your college's policy about student cheating and plagiarism.

newspaper, you will find articles about upcoming events; reports on changes on the college campus; editorials on important student issues; profiles of programs; and advertisements for used books, performances by musical groups, and anything else that students want to announce. The college newspaper is also a forum to explore controversial topics and to discuss sensitive issues.

Newspapers always need students to interview, write, edit, and publish. If you are interested in working for the newspaper, contact the editor or visit a journalism or composition professor.

Bulletin Boards

Even with the increased use of the Internet, the bulletin board is still an important way to get a message to students. Found all over campus, bulletin boards usually advertise used books, needs for roommates and part-time jobs, and upcoming campus events. Bulletin boards within academic buildings often announce four-year university programs, summer workshops, and other types of academic activities.

Classroom Materials

Anything that professors hand out in class is a communication tool. The syllabus is one of the most important documents that you will receive in class, so be sure to read it carefully. In the syllabus you will usually find the following information:

* Instructor's name, office location, phone number, hours open to students, and email address
* Prerequisites for the course
* Course description from the catalog
* Textbook information
* Course objectives, or what you will accomplish by the time you finish the class
* Course content, or what topics will be covered throughout the semester
* Assignments and due dates
* Grading criteria
* Attendance and late-work policies
* Academic integrity statement (which also appears in the student handbook)
* Disability accommodations policy
* General policies for classroom conduct

The syllabus is considered a contract between the student and the instructor. This means that not only will the syllabus contain what is expected of you during class, but it will also contain what you can expect from the instructor. Both of you— the student and the instructor—will be bound by what is stated in the document. Reading the syllabus closely and following it regularly will keep you on top of the policies, expectations, and assignments.

Other essential information that is handed out in class includes directions to assignments, photocopied readings, study questions, and notes. Regard anything that is given to you by the instructor as important, even if you are told "This won't be on the test."

You should also consider the grades and written comments you receive as communication from your instructors. Be sure to read any comments or suggestions that are written on papers and exams, ask questions if you don't understand them or they are illegible, and save all feedback until the semester is over.

College Website

The college's website is where you can find the most current information about classes, academic programs, and contact information for professors. It is easier to update information on a website because it doesn't involve printing and distribution, so it is more likely to provide the most accurate information. College websites usually list phone numbers and email addresses of professors and deans, which makes contacting them easier.

In addition to general information about degrees and departments, your college's website may give you access to professors' syllabi and assignments. This provides a good opportunity to investigate what courses you want to take based on the course objectives and assignments.

PLUS   EXERCISE 5

(Personality + Learning Style = Understanding Situations)

Let's consider Laura's challenge in college: balancing work, family, and college. As she confirms in orientation, she is an aural learner. From what you have learned from this chapter, what should Laura know about transitioning to college full-time that will help ease her mind? What resources could help her be successful?

Now, considering your own learning style, personality type, and special circumstances, what will you do to make the transition to college easier? What have you learned from the chapter that will make the transition smooth for you?

PROFILE

MY STORY
Learning Plan

Directions: Using what you have learned in this chapter and what you know about your learning preferences, choose a task or assignment that needs to be completed soon and create a learning plan that will help you accomplish this task. Then, write your *My Story* Summary, a one-sentence synopsis that crystallizes your newly created plan.

LEARNING TASK	
Time of Day	
Intake Preference	
Social Preference	
Task Management Preference	

MY STORY SUMMARY:

Path of Discovery

What is your experience so far with college culture?
What has been the biggest difference you have experienced
so far between high school or work and college?

HOMEWORK

From College to University

The Changes in Culture and College Services

If you are moving from your community college to a larger, more diverse university, you may experience a slight culture shock despite the semesters you already have under your belt. In addition to a bigger campus with more buildings to find and more students to meet, you may find that a university seems more impersonal. Many students who transfer from a smaller community college complain that professors do not seem to care about them personally and that they lack the support and guidance they received at their other school. Transfer students also note that expectations are higher—and their grades are lower—especially as they move into their majors and begin working toward a career.

Culturally, you should expect that your new university will offer more activities and groups than your smaller community college. You also should expect some kind of adjustment period as you get used to what your new professors expect of you. Statistically, transfer students do experience a slight drop in their GPA. This drop, however, is not necessarily an indication that they were not properly prepared for transfer by their community college.

All in all, the culture shock you experience when transferring to a four-year university will depend on how much bigger and how much more different the school is from your community college. Just remember that whatever differences you notice, there are people at the four-year school who can help you deal with the adjustment. Seek out counselors, advisors, faculty, and students to help make your transition smoother. Your campus map and list of faculty and administrators will point you in the right direction.

From College to Career

How the Culture Will Change Again

Just as you had to adjust to college culture, you will have to make a new adjustment to the workforce if you have never held a full-time job. When starting your first job out of college, you will experience a period of getting used to the way the office or business works. You will encounter new terms, new methods of doing things, and new people. In addition, you will experience working in groups or teams to accomplish tasks, and you will be expected to communicate orally and in a written format. You may also rely more heavily on electronic mail and computers to do your work. Certainly, integrity will be an important part of your working experience. There will be less supervision and more expectation that you do the work you say you will do.

Paying attention to how others act on the job can alleviate any anxiety that you may feel. Just as you made friends and found mentors in college, you should look for others who can offer guidance and help as you learn the ropes of a new career. Also, think about how you adjusted to college and use the same strategies to make your new working environment seem less foreign and more comfortable.

Chapter Review Questions

1. What differences exist between high school and college or a full-time job and college?

2. Name and explain five different characteristics that professors will expect from you as a college student.

3. How and why do colleges grade?

4. What types of documents and communication can you expect in college? What are their purposes?

Case Scenarios

1. In Jennifer's literature class, she is reading Tim O'Brien's *The Things They Carried*. Although she understands that the book is about the Vietnam War, she doesn't know why she has to read a book that contains so much profanity and graphic images of death. She has made an appointment to speak to her professor about the reading assignment because she wants to get out of reading a book that is so depressing and discomforting. What advice would you give Jennifer before she speaks to her professor? Predict what the outcome of the talk will be and what the consequence of the discussion will be on Jennifer's college career.

2. Ja-Ling is taking a biology class. One of her assignments is to create a group presentation on an assigned topic. Her group's topic is the theory of evolution, a theory that Ja-Ling finds fascinating; however, when she meets with her group to prepare for the presentation, two of her group members express deep concern that they are being asked to study something that they don't believe in. They refuse to help with the project even though they know their lack of participation will lower the whole group's grade. What should Ja-Ling do?

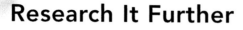

Research It Further

1. Find the University of South Carolina's (USC's) Carolinian Creed on the Internet. Try the website www.sa.sc.edu/CREED/. Using USC's creed as a basis, write your own creed that would fit your college's values. Is there anything that you would revise or add to USC's creed?

2. Find a map of your college and determine what building or landmark is the geographical center of the campus. Then, write a short paper on how that building is an appropriate "center" of your college. Questions you may want to consider include the following: What does the building house—a library? A classroom for the engineering department? A student center? What does the building symbolize? If you were to design a display or piece of art that reflects the "center" of the college, what would it look like?

3. Interview a college employee about his or her job and how it fits into the college's structure. Present the information about the person and the job to your class.

Reference

Banner, J. M., & Cannon, H. C. (1999). *The elements of learning.* New Haven, CT: Yale University Press.

Managing Your Time

2

Managing Your Time

Candace Rowley/Merrill

Laura's Story

Pouring her fourth cup of coffee at 11:00 p.m., Laura searches for her history paper assignment that she copied from the board. It's due at 9 a.m. tomorrow. She sinks into her chair at the kitchen table to go through her backpack one more time and debates whether or not to call a classmate for help. As she begins to tremble from the caffeine, her mind races. Is it too late to call? Will he know how to help her? Laura doesn't normally procrastinate about her school work, but her middle child has been sick for two days and she's been home caring for him and taking him to doctor's appointments. Because of her dyslexia, Laura has taken good notes during class. Her study routine includes recording each lecture, listening to each one repeatedly, and then writing and rewriting what she hears. For information that her professor emphasizes as important, she rewrites her notes in red. Although she still can't find the assignment with the specific requirements, she does have her lecture notes to work with to begin the paper.

At midnight, she is still working. Even though she has downed another cup of coffee, she is tired and her eyes begin to water. She listens to the recorded lecture in which her professor introduces the assignment.

Three hours; two more cups of coffee; a bag of spicy corn nuts; a 68-ounce, fruit-flavored sports drink; and one rerun of *Judge Judy* later, Laura's paper is finished. As she prints her final copy, the printer begins to screech loudly and stops with her last page clutched in its mouth. The ink light blinks at her like her mother's pointing finger saying, "You shouldn't have waited to the last minute, Laura Leigh. This is what happens when you procrastinate."

Frantic, she rips the page from the printer and shakes the ink cartridge in hopes that she can get the last page printed before she hits the bed. When she presses print, the first three words barely appear on the page before the ink completely disappears. The only thing she can do is to save her paper to a thumb drive and hope that tomorrow provides her with a solution.

Exhausted, she shuffles to bed. She sets her alarm an hour earlier so that she can call her mother to come over and watch her son. Before her head reaches the pillow, she remembers a flyer she found for the campus computer lab, which opens at 7 a.m. This may be the solution she was hoping for if she can get to the campus early.

After several hours of deep sleep, Laura has a renewed determination to get the assignment finished and submitted. Because she gets to campus early, she is able to print off the remaining page in the computer lab—thanks to some help from the lab assistant. As she slides into her seat in her history class, she pulls her completed paper out, looks it over one more time, and turns it in. It may not be her best work, she thinks, but it is finished.

"I will return your papers next week," says her professor. He turns to write on the board and says, "In the meantime, you may want to get started on your next paper assignment on Greek culture."

Laura reaches into her backpack, replaces her pen with a red marker, and writes "IMPORTANT" at the top of her page as she copies the assignment from the board.

In This Chapter

In Laura's story, she is feeling the effects of "life getting in the way" as she manages her time and tries to minimize her stress. Would you have done the same as Laura? Would there be anything you would have done differently, either during the same situation or before it even happened? To help you answer those questions, this chapter focuses on the different time and stress management options that can help you stay on task throughout your college career and handle tough situations. Your goal in reading this chapter will be to find the method that works best for you and that helps you keep time and stress more manageable. Specifically, you will be able to:

* Determine what steps are needed to get organized.

* Consider different time management strategies.

* Examine goals and priorities as they relate to time management.

* Explain how your energy levels are an important part of time management.

* Identify time and energy zappers.

* Identify strategies to eliminate procrastination.

* Recognize methods for minimizing stress at work, home, and college.

Is Time on Your Side?

Is it surprising that the number one issue that community college students say is their biggest challenge is **time management?** Why do so many students identify time management as one of the areas that they need more help with? The answer may be that for many of them, they are adding another responsibility to their busy lives. Another answer could be that they are now expected to do things they haven't done before or haven't done for a long time. Being a student demands more than just showing up for class. There is plenty of work to do outside of class—at home, in the library, on the computer, and in study groups. Being aware of how you spend your time and choosing the most effective strategies for you will not only help you complete more tasks in a *timely manner,* but will also help you minimize the stress that comes from trying to juggle many responsibilities.

The benefits of managing time effectively include not only getting tasks completed, but also experiencing the success of accomplishment. Darwin B. Nelson and Gary R. Low (2003), in their book *Emotional Intelligence: Achieving Academic and Career Excellence,* state that "[a]n important by-product of good Time Management is a feeling of self-control—we are managing our responsibilities, not being managed by them" (pp. 100–101). You will certainly feel more in control of your time after you complete this chapter!

Getting Organized

The first aspect to consider when it comes to managing your time and stress is getting organized. Seems like a simple idea, but think about how much time you have wasted before when you couldn't find something or how you missed an important event because you didn't write it down. Nothing is more stressful than knowing you could have done better if you had been organized! Getting organized for success, however, doesn't have to take a lot of money and time. If you use a few simple strategies, you can save yourself both time and energy in the long run. To help get organized, think of the three S's: Supplies, Space, and Same Time. The three **S's** consists of getting the right **supplies** (including a calendar), keeping your **space** clean and organized, and checking your "to do list" or calendar at the **same time** each day.

Supplies for Success

Pens, pencils, calculators, paper, notebooks, and thumb drives, oh my! There are so many items you will need in college to get organized and complete assignments—not including books, lab manuals, and computer access. What you *need* will depend on what you are taking and what your instructors' expectations are. What you *want* to get in addition will depend on your preferences and your budget. At the very least, a good, sturdy backpack that can accommodate all your books and notebooks—and that doesn't break your back—should be high on your supply list.

Many a good student has fallen victim to "assignment amnesia." This disorder occurs when otherwise smart students believe they can remember all of their assignments and appointments without writing them down and without consulting their syllabi or course outlines. Fortunately, there are measures you can take to prevent an attack of assignment amnesia: using a calendar or a device, like a cell phone, that keeps track of your assignments, especially one in which you also add all the tasks you need to complete from your personal, professional, and college life.

If you use a paper calendar, you have many different types from which to choose. Once you determine the type that works best for you—a monthly, weekly, or daily calendar—make a habit of writing down your tasks, no matter how big or small. Here is an example of a typical list of a day's activities for a student like Laura:

THURSDAY

* Make appointment to have oil changed
* Pick up medicine for Terrence
* Take Phillip to baseball
* Study for history quiz on Friday
* Read 30 pages for English
* Get book from library

A typical monthly calendar, as Exhibit 1 shows, allows you to see several weeks at once so that you can remain aware of upcoming events, but often there is little space on a monthly calendar to write down detailed lists such as the one above.

A weekly calendar, such as the one in Exhibit 2, allows you to glance at one week at a time. A benefit to a weekly calendar is that you have room to write details of each activity; however, a drawback to a weekly calendar is that it is difficult to anticipate what you must do the next week.

Daily calendars usually provide the most space to write your day-to-day tasks and appointments. This kind of calendar may be the most difficult to work with if you need to plan ahead. Because you cannot see the rest of the week or month, you may overlook important events or be surprised by them. Use a daily calendar, like

EXHIBIT 1   Lightly Scheduled Monthly Calendar

SUNDAY	MONDAY	TUESDAY	WEDNESDAY	THURSDAY	FRIDAY	SATURDAY
					1	2
3	4	5	6	7	8	9 picnic—noon
10	11 work late	12	13	14	15 pay bills	16
17	18	19	20	21 play rehearsal 7:00	22	23
24	25 nutrition exam 10:00	26	27	28	29	30 birthday party 2:00

EXHIBIT 2   Heavily Scheduled Weekly Calendar

MONDAY	TUESDAY	WEDNESDAY	THURSDAY	FRIDAY	SATURDAY	SUNDAY
8:30 Work	9:00 English	8:30 Work	9:00 English	8:30 Work	8–10 Clean house	3–8 Work on paper
2:00 Geology	11:00 Acct.	2:00 Geology	11:00 Acct.	2:00 Geology	3–4 Exercise	
3:00 Trig	6:00 Help sister with painting	3:00 Trig		3:00 Trig	6–11 Study	
5:00 Pick up dinner				7:00 Movie with friend		
7:00 Study for Accounting						

the one in Exhibit 3, if you are extremely organized and can plan ahead effectively, or use it in addition to a monthly calendar.

Space Considerations

The right stuff and the ideal calendar are first steps to managing your time well, but there is more you can do. To manage your time effectively and efficiently, create a clutter-free space where you can study and complete assignments. If you don't have a place in your house or apartment that you can call your own, a comfortable chair or seat at the kitchen table may be all that you can spare. Make sure it is comfortable and quiet and has adequate space for books, notebooks, and other supplies. It has to be a place where you *want* to be or it will be difficult to go there to stay on task.

EXHIBIT 3   Daily Calendar

FRIDAY
MARCH 12, 2010

7:00	Wake up, shower, get ready for school
8:00	Drive to school, arrive early, study in the library
9:00	College Algebra
10:00	English 2
11:00	Study for Biology exam
12:00	Eat lunch and review notes for College Algebra
1:00	Biology—EXAM!!
2:00	Drive to work
3:00	Work
4:00	Work
5:00	Work

Same Time, Same Place

A good system for writing down your daily tasks and establishing a place to complete your assignments are a good foundation to managing your time well and reducing the negative effects of stress. However, there is one last tip: Create a routine. In other words, every evening write down your goals for the next day and every morning review what you need to do for the day. Knowing what to expect for the day will make surprises less likely. As you complete each task, scratch it off the list. You will get the satisfaction of a completed job and can focus on the next task.

Making Time for College

How much time should you devote to college? Some first-time students seriously underestimate the amount of time that is needed to prepare for a class, study for tests, and complete assignments. Unfortunately, they often realize their error when an assignment is due or a test is given. A common formula for calculating the amount of study time is to multiply the number of credit hours for the course by three. For example, a demanding class that carries three credit hours and meets three times per week for 1 hour each time will require 9 hours per week of out-of-class work. These 9 hours plus the 3 hours in class means you will spend a total of 12 hours studying and attending that one class each week. Multiply 12 hours by 4 classes and you will have a 48-hour college work week. Add 40 hours of work on the job and you will be spending 88 hours per week working on your job and your classes!

EXHIBIT 4   Student College Schedule

RESPONSIBILITY	CONTACT HOURS PER WEEK	OUTSIDE HOURS PER WEEK	TOTAL HOURS PER WEEK
College Algebra	3	6–9	9–12
Composition 101	3	6–9	9–12
U.S. History	3	6–9	9–12
Reading	3	6–9	9–12
Work	25		25

Total Hours per Week: 61–73 Hours

Looking at Exhibit 4 can be overwhelming for students, especially if they work more than 25 hours and take more than 12 credit hours per semester. A full-time student who also works full time can expect to spend half her hours a week working on classes or at work (and that doesn't include time to sleep!). Studies have shown that the reality of how much time students spend outside of class is much lower than the recommended number of hours, but students often find that how much time they spend varies from semester to semester, depending on what kinds of classes they take.

To see how the recommended study hours look when they are scheduled throughout the week, check out Laura's calendar in Exhibit 5. She works full-time, a 40-hour week, and is in class 12 hours each week.

Given Laura's schedule in Exhibit 5, will she be able to reach the 48 hours that are needed to take and study for college classes? If she were to add two hours a night after class—and if she felt like studying after a long day—she would study an additional 10 hours during the work week, which leaves 22 hours and 15 minutes of studying to be completed in her "spare time."

Look at the calendar again. In order to reach 48 hours of studying and class, where will Laura include additional study time? Will she need to study every waking moment that she is not at work, in class, or taking care of herself and her other responsibilities? If she could not devote that much time to her college classes, would Laura need to take fewer classes, ask for help with home responsibilities, or cut back on her hours at work? Despite what some may think, Laura doesn't have to give up her dream to be in college, but she will need to rearrange her schedule. Without doing so, she will not be able to meet the demands of her classes. However, she can feel some comfort in knowing that getting up a little earlier, multitasking, and using her weekends for studying at longer intervals will be short-term changes to her schedule.

But What Do I Do?

The question sometimes arises as to what you should be doing for those 6–9 hours each week. For one, you will need to read any assigned material *before* class. Another activity that will need to be part of your outside study time is reviewing your notes

EXHIBIT 5   Laura's Weekly Calendar

MONDAY	TUESDAY	WEDNESDAY	THURSDAY	FRIDAY	SATURDAY	SUNDAY
6:30–7:30 Get ready for school	6:30–7:30 Get ready for school	6:30–7:30 Get ready for school	6:30–7:30 Get ready for school	6:30–7:30 Get ready for school	7:00–10:00 Clean house, shop	7:00–10:00 Study
7:30–7:45 Travel to work	7:30–7:45 Travel to work	7:30–7:45 Travel to work	7:30–7:45 Travel to work	7:30–7:45 Travel to work	10:00–11:30 Soccer	10:00–11:00 Go to church
8:00–12:30 Work	8:00–12:30 Work	8:00–12:30 Work	8:00–12:30 Work	8:00–12:30 Work	11:30–12:15 Lunch with team	11:15–12:30 Lunch with parents
12:30–1:15 Eat lunch and run errands	12:30–1:15 Go to doctor's appointment	12:30–1:15 Eat lunch with friend	12:30–1:15 Eat lunch and walk 1 mile	12:30–1:15 Eat lunch and study	12:15–2:00 Run errands	12:45–3:45 Study
1:15–4:45 Work	1:15–4:45 Work	1:15–4:45 Work	1:15–4:45 Work	1:15–4:45 Work	2:00–6:00 Go to library and do research	3:45–5:45 Do yard work
4:45–5:00 Travel	4:45–5:00 Travel	4:45–5:00 Travel	4:45–5:00 Travel	4:45–5:00 Travel	6:00–7:00 Fix and eat dinner	6:00–7:00 Eat dinner
5:00–5:45 Eat dinner and study	5:00–5:45 Eat dinner and study	5:00–5:45 Eat dinner and study	5:00–5:45 Eat dinner and study	5:00–7:00 Eat dinner with friends	7:00–9:00 Study	7:00–8:00 Walk 3 miles
6:00–9:30 Classes	6:00–9:30 Classes	6:00–9:30 Classes	6:00–9:30 Classes	7:00–9:30 See movie	9:00–10:00 Answer email and watch TV	8:00–10:00 Do laundry, get ready for next week
10:00 Go to bed	10:00 Go to bed	10:00 Go to bed	10:00 Go to bed	10:00 Go to bed	10:00 Go to bed	10:00 Go to bed

from class and filling in any gaps in information that you were not able to get by working with a classmate. Rewriting your notes after the discussion of the chapter or topic is another very important way you can spend an hour for the week. Of course, you will need to budget time to complete assignments, whether they are review questions at the end of a chapter or a research project.

The plan in Exhibit 6 is for *one* college class. If you have more than one, you will need to add an hour each day of the week for each 3-credit-hour class that you are taking.

EXHIBIT 6   One-Hour-a-Day Time Management Plan

DAY OF THE WEEK	TIME	ASSIGNMENT	COMPLETED	
Sunday	3:30–4:30 p.m.	Read Chapter 5 and take notes while reading. Review notes after reading the chapter once.	Yes	No
Monday	7:00–8:00 p.m.	Review reading notes as well as class notes. Define all vocabulary terms that are key to the chapter and that are unfamiliar.	Yes	No
Tuesday	11:15–12:15 p.m.	Answer study questions that accompany the chapter.	Yes	No
Wednesday	8:00–9:00 p.m.	Create sample test questions on flash cards and write the answers on the back.	Yes	No
Thursday	7:00–8:00 p.m.	Complete homework questions for the chapter.	Yes	No
Friday	5:30–6:00 a.m. and 3:30–4:00 p.m.	Review flash cards.	Yes	No
Saturday	3:30–4:30 p.m.	Rewrite notes from the entire week of class. Include any material that was assigned in the reading but not covered in class.	Yes	No

Even with the best intentions, many students, however, opt to cut back on studying because the other activities, such as running errands and participating in their children's activities, are necessary parts of their lives and cannot be eliminated or rearranged. Realistically, you may be able to cut back on studying in some classes at slower times; however, you should not eliminate study hours for all classes throughout each semester. Your best bet is to recognize that taking college classes is a tremendous time commitment and to work your other responsibilities (except maintaining your health) around them as best you can. You won't always be able to put college as your first priority, but you will need to make a conscious effort to put studying near the top of your list most of the time.

Managing Your Time

Despite our many differences, what we all have in common is that we have the same number of hours each day and the same number of days each week. Why, then, does it seem as though some people are more accomplished than others? Are they able to magically extend the day by a few hours or sneak eight days into a week? Do they forgo all sleep, meals, and personal needs just to get things done? We would like to believe that high achievers have superhuman strength, but the truth is they usually do not do anything to achieve their goals that we cannot do as well. When you talk to very productive people, they usually tell you that the secret to their success is that they have learned to manage their time efficiently. Effective time management is not a talent; it is a skill, one that gets better as you practice over time.

EXHIBIT 7   Time Log Example

TIME	WEDNESDAY'S ACTIVITIES
7:00 a.m.	Get ready for classes; eat breakfast
7:30 a.m.	Review notes for business class
8:00 a.m.	En route to school
8:30 a.m.	Business Communications
9:00 a.m.	Class, continued
9:30 a.m.	Class, continued
10:00 a.m.	See advisor to plan next semester's classes

Analyzing Your Time

After recognizing that we all have the same number of hours, analyzing your time is another step to effective time management. Tim Hindle (1998), in his book *Manage Your Time,* suggests keeping a time log of your day that is divided into 30-minute increments (p. 9). Separate from your calendar, the purpose of a 30-minute time log is to help raise your awareness of what you are doing throughout the day. You can make your own time log like the one in Exhibit 7 and keep up with one day's worth of activities, but be sure to give yourself time to write down your activities either every few hours or at the end of the day. Keeping an eye on how you spend your time will help you make realistic time management goals and will keep you from wasting too much time or miscalculating how much time it takes you to complete tasks.

Asking the questions "Where did the time go?" and "What do I do with my time?" is a start to analyzing your time. You will also need to analyze your time management skills—or how well you use your time wisely to meet your goals and stay healthy in the process. The assessment in Activity 1 asks 10 questions about time management abilities.

Back-Dating Time Management Plan

If there is one piece of advice that experienced students want to pass along to new students that would help them manage their time better, it is that even though they sound the same when spoken aloud, the words "due" and "do" *don't* mean the same thing. Starting the night before an assignment is due may create more stress than is necessary. Therefore, the method of creating "do" dates before

Critical Thinking

EXERCISE 1

Look at all the calendars and time management strategies in this chapter. Which ones seem to be easier for you to use? What are the characteristics that make the calendars easier or harder for you to use?

PRACTICE

ACTIVITY 1   Personal Time Assessment

Circle the number (1—Never, 2—Sometimes, 3—Usually, 4—Always) that best describes your experience.

STATEMENT	NEVER	SOMETIMES	USUALLY	ALWAYS
1. I arrive at class prepared.	1	2	3	4
2. I review my notes within 24 hours of class.	1	2	3	4
3. I spend my time on campus taking care of personal business, talking with professors, studying, or doing research.	1	2	3	4
4. I have study goals, and I achieve them each week.	1	2	3	4
5. I feel prepared for tests.	1	2	3	4
6. I spend enough time on writing assignments.	1	2	3	4
7. I get enough sleep each night.	1	2	3	4
8. I spend some time each week doing something I enjoy.	1	2	3	4
9. I have enough time to take care of most of my personal needs.	1	2	3	4
10. I get support from others to help me meet my educational goals.	1	2	3	4
Score each column.				
Add each column's total.				Total

SCORE RANGE	MEANING
40–32	You do a good job of managing your time. For the most part, you are satisfied with how you manage your time and what you accomplish each week.
31–26	You are doing a good job managing your time for most activities. Identify your weaker areas and create a plan to improve time management in those areas.
25–19	You may be dissatisfied with your time management and find only a few goals are met each week. Review what you are doing right with some of your time and make a plan that will draw upon your time management strengths.
Below 18	You may feel as though you are not meeting the majority of your goals during the week. An honest look at your goals, your necessary activities, and your priorities is needed.

EXHIBIT 8   Back-Dating Time Management

SUNDAY	MONDAY	TUESDAY	WEDNESDAY	THURSDAY	FRIDAY	SATURDAY
		1	2	3	4	5
6	7	8 1:00 p.m. Receive paper assignment	9 6–7:30 p.m. Choose paper topic; brainstorm or freewrite on topic	10	11 9–10:30 p.m. Reread brainstorming list; create a draft outline	12
13 3–5:00 p.m. Write first draft of paper	14	15 11–12:00 noon Visit writing lab for assistance with paper	16	17	18 8:30–10:30 p.m. Write second draft of paper, incorporating tutor's advice	19
20 3–4:30 p.m. Write final draft of paper	21	22	23 8–9:00 p.m. Edit paper; print on quality paper; place in backpack	24 2:00 p.m. Turn in paper	25	26
27	28	29	30			

your assignment is "due," or back-dating assignments, is an essential one to use if you are going to create habits of completing assignments successfully. To see how this works, let's say you have a career exploration paper that is due on the 24th of this month (see Exhibit 8). In order to build enough time into your schedule, you can use a calendar to divide the possible steps to your paper and fill in the calendar with the time that you have to work on the paper. When back-dating assignment tasks, remember to provide adequate time between tasks so that you can reflect on the work that you have done and approach the assignment with "fresh eyes" each time.

Making Time for Relationships

No doubt you are getting the connection between college success and time management. A good relationship with at least one person at your college can mean the difference between completing a degree and dropping out. Then, it should be no surprise that cultivating and maintaining good relationships takes time and takes making time to work on them. Experienced students will tell you that when they were new students they underestimated how much time they would need to devote to meeting with advisors, counselors, and professors outside of class. Some think that unless there is an academic problem, they will not need to see their professors regularly during their office hours. Nothing could be farther from the truth: If your goal is to make solid connections during the semester with your professors, you will need more time than just before class or right after. Moreover, if you find that you will need to work closely with a counselor or tutor, you will have to find enough time during the week to make that happen. Some students schedule their classes and work or family obligations with so little wiggle room that substantial amounts of time to get extra help or to plan out their degrees are nonexistent.

With this said, it is a good idea to look at your schedule now (and consider this when you plan for next semester) and see what days and times work best for meeting with people on campus. Try to keep those times free and clear in case you need to use them at the last minute. If you find you do not need that time that day to take care of personal business on campus or to talk to your professor, then you have a little extra time that can be used for studying, completing assignments, or even relaxing a bit. It is hard to make any relationship work if you don't spend enough time nurturing it; likewise, relationships in college, whether they are with professors, counselors, advisors, or fellow classmates, need time to develop. The benefits of taking the time to cultivate strong relationships are endless and can certainly help you stay on course and possibly provide you with new opportunities for connections you couldn't have imagined.

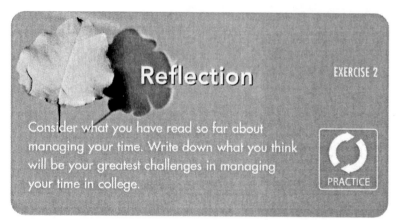

Reflection   EXERCISE 2

Consider what you have read so far about managing your time. Write down what you think will be your greatest challenges in managing your time in college.

PRACTICE

Managing Your Priorities

Managing your time and priorities when you are in college can be a game of strategy, action, and patience. In the following exercise, consider what should be top priority; what can be completed if there is time; and what can be delegated, modified, or rescheduled for another day.

It is Monday morning and you have 10 items on your "to do" list (Exhibit 9) that you would like to get accomplished today, but you don't have enough time to complete all the items. Determine which activities are top priorities and which are not. Then, list what you have eliminated from the list and explain why you decided to make it a low priority item. Finally, describe how you will accomplish the low priority items the next day.

From the list in Exhibit 9, determine what three items should be top priority.

Top Priority _____

Top Priority _____

Top Priority _____

Why did you determine these priorities to be the most important?

_____

_____

With the time remaining, determine what else can be accomplished in the same day.

Additional activity _____

Additional activity _____

EXHIBIT 9   To Do List

MONDAY'S TO DO LIST—FOURTH WEEK OF CLASSES

- Pick up sister from airport at 7:30 p.m. (Airport is 15 minutes away.)

- Attend two classes, one at 2:00 p.m. and one at 4:00 p.m. (You have a one-hour b... between.)

- Complete paper for 4:00 class. (You will need an hour to finish.)

- Prepare dinner for family at 6:30 p.m. (It will take at least 30 minutes.)

- Study for Tuesday's psychology exam. (You would like to spend two hours.)

- Take children to school at 7:45 a.m. (School is 10 minutes from your house.)

- Get up at 6:00 a.m. and go to gym for an hour's workout.

- Call your cousin who had surgery last week. (30 minutes)

- Help children with homework. (1 hour)

- Meet study group at noon to start working on final project in business communications class.

Additional activity _____

Additional activity _____

Why did you determine that the above activities could be completed if time allowed?

_____

_____

What items can be low priority, modified, or rescheduled?

Low priority _____

Low priority _____

Low priority _____

Why did you choose these items as low priority?

_____

_____

How could you modify the low-priority items so that they could be completed in the same day?

_____

_____

Before you can begin to manage your time, you will need to make sure that your goals and priorities are clear. Writing down your goals and setting your priorities, which may change frequently, are the first steps to realizing your dreams; they are also the first steps to figuring out how much time you need to spend on each goal. Before you can think about time management, take time to review what you have written down as your short-term goals and priorities.

If you were to list your priorities right now, college would be near the top of the list. Certainly, your enrolling in college and reading this text mean that you are committed to furthering your education. Nevertheless, you will need to figure out where the priority of going to college fits in with your other priorities. Perhaps attending classes is your only priority because you live alone and do not work; more likely, however, college will compete with other priorities. If you are going to succeed in college, your education must be a top priority the majority of the time.

In addition to college, you may need to consider your family as a priority. Depending on your situation, you may have family members who need you for emotional, physical, and financial support. You may even be the only one they can rely on. Because family is often a first priority for many students, it will be important to manage your time with them wisely and effectively.

If you have not done so yet, you should talk to your family about the new responsibilities that you will have. Be honest in your descriptions of what you will be doing and what you will need from them. If you think your time will be limited for family trips and weekend activities, let them know. If you think you will need to cut out some basic duties such as planning meals, cleaning the house, and running errands, be sure to communicate this to your family. The more they know about what to expect, the better able they will be to support your decision to enroll in college.

Time is valuable only if you plan and use it well.

Stephen Derr/Getty Images Inc.–Image Bank

Another priority that you may have is your job. Most community college students work as well as attend classes. For some, their jobs supplement their household income and are not necessary for survival; for many others, their jobs are more important than college because they provide the primary or sole income for the family. If your job is your top priority, then you should know where the other priorities must fall, and you should be prepared to make sacrifices in other areas to ensure that your job remains at the top.

With all the other responsibilities you have, it is easy to overlook the priority of relaxing; without it, the other priorities can run you down. Don't forget that you can have fun while in college, and you certainly want to allow yourself to participate in activities that you enjoy. Without them, your college career will seem stressful and dull. Scheduling "down time" to play and rejuvenate will be an important part of effective time management. Get outside, read for pleasure, or participate in the types of activities you enjoy. Relaxing and having fun will recharge your body and mind to concentrate on the demands of your other priorities.

Managing Your Energy

Just as important as managing your time is managing your energy. Think about this scenario: You have all weekend off from work and your spouse has taken the kids to visit their grandparents. Therefore, you have 48 hours of complete solitude to write a research paper that is due on Monday. Sounds ideal, doesn't it? But what if you have the flu for those two days? Does the time mean anything when you don't have the energy to do any work? What if, instead of having the flu, you pulled two double shifts and haven't slept more than 5 hours in two days? Will you be able to use your free 48 hours productively or will you need to take care of yourself?

Time, in other words, is only valuable if you have the energy to use it well. Thus, you need to be aware of how you feel, how energetic you are, and how willing you are to use your time wisely. To determine which times of the day you feel the most energetic, place an "X" in the appropriate column of Activity 2 for each time of day. If you work nights and sleep during most of the day, create your own chart with the times that you are awake.

In addition to the time of day, your energy levels rise and fall during the week. Do you find yourself tired on Monday mornings, but full of energy on Fridays? Or do you feel worn out by Thursday evenings, but rejuvenated on Sundays? Depending

ACTIVITY 2   Time of Day Energy Levels

TIME OF DAY	HIGH ENERGY	NEUTRAL	LOW ENERGY
6:00 a.m.			
8:00 a.m.			
10:00 a.m.			
12 noon			
2:00 p.m.			
4:00 p.m.			
6:00 p.m.			
8:00 p.m.			
10:00 p.m.			
12 midnight			

Day of Week Energy Levels

	HIGH ENERGY	NEUTRAL	LOW ENERGY
Sunday			
Monday			
Tuesday			
Wednesday			
Thursday			
Friday			
Saturday			

on your work, school, and personal schedules, you will find that you have regular bursts of energy at certain times of the week. To determine which days of the week you feel most energetic, write an "X" in the appropriate columns in Activity 3.

Identifying Time and Energy Zappers

Despite your best efforts in managing your time and energy, there will be times when you find your best-laid plans are interrupted by needy people and last-minute changes in plans. A few distractions during the day can be a nice break from the mundane tasks of going to school and working or caring for a family. However, if they take so much time away from your studies that you can't seem to keep up with the pace of your classes or that you are stressed out, you will need to find ways to lessen the frequency of or eliminate the intrusions altogether.

You may be able to create your own list of time and energy zappers, but here are a few common ones:

* People who want your attention and time, but who don't need it
* Interruptions such as unnecessary phone calls
* Fatigue and illness
* Personal problems
* Mindless television watching
* Internet surfing that serves no purpose
* Continuous "chatting" online
* Playing video or computer games
* Inability to say "no"
* Procrastination
* Poor organization
* Inability to concentrate because of learning difficulty, medication, or stress

Now is the time to block out the zappers. You won't be able to afford the time that they waste, and you will need to be proactive in getting rid of them. Some will be easy to reduce or get rid of, such as playing video games or hanging out all day with friends; others will be more difficult, such as learning to say "no" to people or eliminating procrastination. The key to getting rid of the energy and time wasters is to take on the easiest ones and work on the others through goal setting. Of course, one person's time waster is another person's stress reliever. If you find that playing a video game or going to a movie with friends is necessary to refresh yourself before tackling other important tasks, schedule it as part of your weekly routine. When those activities keep you from finishing others, then it may be time to reassess how often you do them.

One way to help yourself manage your energy is by becoming aware of what activities relax you when you are stressed and what activities allow you to refill your energy reserves. In Activity 4, place an "X" in the appropriate column next to each activity. If the activity does both, place an "X" in both columns. If the activity neither relaxes nor energizes, then leave both columns blank. Use this chart when planning your time. If an activity rejuvenates you, helps you recharge, you may want

ACTIVITY 4   Time and Energy Zappers

ACTIVITY	RELAXING	ENERGIZING
Watching television		
Spending time with family/friends		
Pleasure reading		
Doing housework		
Exercising (light to moderate)		
Gardening		
Talking on the phone		
Writing		
Cooking		
Shopping		
Napping		
Participating in a hobby		
Surfing the Internet		
Organizing closets, drawers, files		
Enjoying a nice meal		

Working within a group or with another classmate, describe the types of activities that can zap students' time and energy, then create solutions for managing them. Present your ideas to the class.

EXERCISE 3

to schedule times to do it when you need more energy. If an activity helps you wind down, you may want to schedule it after you have completed major tasks.

Running Low on Time and Energy

There will be times when you find yourself with goals for the day or week still left on your list, but you don't have the time and energy reserves that you hoped to have. Sometimes life throws us a curveball, and our beautiful plans are mangled if not completely destroyed. If you find yourself in such a situation, then you will benefit from changing goals and priorities quickly and eliminating unnecessary items from your "to do" list. For example, you had planned to bake a friend a birthday cake from scratch, but you don't have two hours to do it. What can you do? How about buying a cake on the way to your friend's house? The outcome is still the same: Your friend has a cake for his birthday. You hoped to get all the bills paid by the end of the day, but you don't have the time and energy left? Pay the bills that are due the soonest and complete the task the next day.

There will be some days that you just can't do it all. You may find that you cannot read the assigned chapter in your sociology class the night before. If this happens to you—and it will at some time in your college career—then create a back-up plan like the ones offered above. Avoid giving up completely if you run out of time or energy; do something, even if it is just a little bit. Can't get to the library to start looking for sources for your research paper? Create an outline or a task list instead, and go to the library the next day. Do something that keeps you moving forward, but don't give up. You will have more energy and time the next day to complete new tasks.

Putting Procrastination in Its Place

One would think that all college students routinely participate in cramming and "pulling all-nighters." Putting off studying and completing projects will certainly add to your stress, but procrastination does not have to be a necessary part of going to college. Realistically, community college students probably delay beginning projects and studying because they are pressed for time, not because they are wasting time hanging out with their friends or goofing off. However, in order to maximize your time, you can follow the same rules as for procrastinators.

There are many humorous sayings about procrastination:

"If it weren't for the last minute, nothing would get done." —Anonymous
"I never put off till tomorrow what I can possibly do . . . the day after." —Oscar Wilde

Kidding aside, procrastination can be, American author Elbert Hubbard remarked, "the father of failure." Postponing an activity or task because you do not want to do it or can find more interesting activities to do can have serious consequences. For example, if you put off researching your legal terminology paper until the night before, you might find that the library has closed early or the access to online databases is down. You may even discover, like Laura, that your computer won't work and your printer is out of ink.

Procrastination can be the barrier between you and your goals, and it can cause you undue stress. Managing your time and planning ahead will, however, minimize the likelihood that you will procrastinate. Writing down your tasks and goals, too, will make them visible and instill the joy of crossing them off your list.

FIGHTING PROCRASTINATION

* Create a time line of when you want to complete each part of your project. Make adjustments if needed, but try to stick to the schedule.

* Give yourself enough time to complete each part. It is easy to assume that you can find all the resources you need for a paper in one day, for example. A more realistic goal is to find two sources during one trip to the library.

* Just do it. Start right here, right now, and don't think about finding a better time to begin.

* Recognize that behind every procrastinator is someone who fears—the unknown or failure. Acknowledge that fear by writing down what the fear is. Once you recognize your fear, you are more likely to move past it.

* Reward yourself for completing a particularly difficult or boring project.

* Write a list of consequences for *not* doing the project on time and a list of consequences for doing the project on time. Decide which list you can live with.

* Remind yourself of the reason that you are in college and think about how this project supports that reason.

Critical Thinking

EXERCISE 4

Using what you have learned about your energy levels, your priorities, and your stressors, as well as the exercises you completed in this chapter, create a plan for handling stress over the next week and schedule your "stress-relieving" tasks on a calendar that works best for you.

PRACTICE

INTEGRITY MATTERS

One way to eliminate stress and anxiety is to make integrity a top priority. Even though it may seem less stressful to take the easier path, in the long run, your negative stress will be less when you maintain your integrity.

PLUS

(Personality + Learning Style = Understanding Situations)

Let's revisit Laura's dilemma. She is an aural learner and introverted; she also takes longer to complete assignments because of her dyslexia; and she has to juggle family and college because she is a single parent. What time and stress management strategies can she use the next time that she has an assignment due?

Now, considering your own learning style, personality type, and special circumstances, what would you do to avoid the stress of completing an assignment the night before when you find yourself challenged by unexpected events?

PROFILE

MY STORY
Learning Plan

Directions: Using what you have learned in this chapter and what you know about your learning preferences, choose a task or assignment that needs to be completed soon and create a learning plan that will help you accomplish this task. Then, write your *My Story* Summary, a one-sentence synopsis that crystallizes your newly created plan.

PROFILE

LEARNING TASK	
Time of Day	
Intake Preference	
Social Preference	
Task Management Preference	

MY STORY SUMMARY:

Path of Discovery

Journal Entry

What energizes you the most? What could you do for hours and not notice that time has passed? Describe the activity and discuss why you think you find so much pleasure in the activity that you don't mind spending time doing it.

HOMEWORK

From College to University

How to Handle the New Pressures on Your Time

A good time management strategy that works now for you will serve you well when you transfer to a university. Yes, there will be more work and more expected of you when you get closer to completing a bachelor's degree, but there may also be less direction from professors. They will assume you have solid time management skills. The more you practice now, the better you will be able to handle even more restrictions on your time. Try out a few strategies and find what works, but also talk to students who have already transferred to find out what new expectations you will encounter.

From College to Career

Improving Time Management on the Job

If you decide to go directly from college to work, or back to work, your time management skills can be the difference between a dreaded job and a life-fulfilling career. Time management will be even more important on the job because your actions will affect more people. Just like a move from college to university, the more you practice good time management skills, the more likely you will be able to complete assignments on time. Beware, though, that on the job, the stakes will be much higher than they were in college. Using a calendar and writing down daily tasks will help you keep up with your work. Also, being honest about *not* meeting deadlines will keep you on top (and will help minimize stress). There may be times when you won't be able to manage your time as effectively as you wish, but if you can be honest and speak up quickly, you may be able to save others time as well.

Chapter Review Questions

1. What should you consider when you begin working out a time management plan for a semester?

2. What stresses you? In what ways can you eliminate or reduce the amount of stress that you have?

3. What activities zap your time, and what can you do to eliminate the amount of time they take from you?

4. What strategies are available to eliminate procrastination?

Case Scenarios

1. Janice has been doing very well in her classes. She has been able to manage her time wisely and adjust her schedule any time something unexpected has come up. However, Janice has had a hectic week. Her boss expects her to stay late for the week to finish a special project; she has an important exam on Thursday evening; her daughter has been sick with a stomach virus; and her husband has been out of town for the last two weeks. Her goal is to take care of each problem without jeopardizing her job, her grade, or her daughter's welfare. What do you recommend she do? Is it realistic that she can take care of each of her problems?

2. George has a 20-page research paper in his Abnormal Psychology class due at the end of the semester. The professor has asked for an annotated bibliography, an outline, and a rough draft to be turned in at the same time as the final draft. George is feeling overwhelmed. Help him map out a plan of action so that he can fulfill his requirements without unnecessary stress.

3. Barbara has been sick for two weeks and has fallen behind in her classes. She is worried that she won't be able to catch up or that she will not be allowed to make up her work. What should she do?

Research It Further

1. Keep a journal of how you spend your time for the next seven days. Write down how long you spend on each activity. Make sure you are honest and that you write in your journal every few hours. Then, create a report for your class as to how you spend the majority of your time.

2. Create a survey that asks your classmates how students spend their time. Once you collect your data, report the results to your class and determine which activities are most prominent among students.

3. Create a "toolbox" for students who are plagued by procrastination. Make the toolbox creative and fun.

References

Hindle, T. (1998). *Manage your time.* New York: DK Publishing.

Nelson, D. B., & Low, G. R. (2003). *Emotional intelligence: Achieving academic and career excellence.* Upper Saddle River, NJ: Pearson.

Listening and Taking Notes Effectively

3

From Chapter 8 of *The Community College Experience Plus,* Second Edition, Amy Baldwin.
Copyright © 2010 by Pearson Education, Inc. Published by Pearson Prentice Hall. All rights reserved.

Listening and Taking Notes Effectively

Laura's Story

Laura settles in her usual seat in the front row of her world civilization class. After the lesson she learned about writing down important information when she is in class, Laura has gotten better about listening more closely even when distractions compete for her attention.

"The clip we are about to watch," her professor says as she pushes the play button on the television's DVD player, "discusses the ancient library in Timbuktu."

Laura laughs at herself as she tries to spell Timbuktu. She underlines the word so that she can remember to go back and check the spelling when she rewrites her notes. Having dyslexia is frustrating at times, but she has found that laughing about her challenges is a great way to relieve her stress in certain situations.

"I love it when she stops lecturing and shows us these videos," her classmate next to her whispers in her ear. Laura misses some of the information in the video because of the distraction, but makes another note to fill in the missing information later. She loves how engaging the films are, but her dyslexia makes it difficult for her to watch and take notes.

"Hey? Do you have an extra pen?" her classmate whispers again. She knows his name, Franco, because he is a friend of Juanita's, but she hasn't talked to him much. He seems more interested in socializing than paying attention in class.

She hands him a pen and makes another note to fill in any gaps she has from being distracted. Laura is not too worried about the missing information because she has been able to view a few of the clips on her own—the library has a copy of everything her professor uses in class—but even watching them over and over again is sometimes challenging despite her comfort with learning by listening.

As the lights come back on, her professor asks if there are any questions.

"Yeah, I have one. Will that be on the test? I mean, are we responsible for remembering everything that guy said?" asks someone from the back of the room.

"Sure. You have the material that was assigned for reading, the information I cover in the lecture, and then anything else that I bring in. All of this should be studied for the test," the professor says.

"And she's not lying," says Laura to herself. Even with help from her mentor and the tutor in the learning assistance center, Laura has her work cut out for her: The information in the book is arranged chronologically, but her professor lectures on causes and effects in history, constantly referencing other eras, people, and dates in the process. Then, there are the tests that cover major themes such as important reformers or federal policies. No one note-taking strategy seems to work for reading, listening, and studying.

"Any other questions?" her professor asks and pauses for a few seconds. "Okay, if you realize you do have questions after class, be sure to email me or come by my office early next week. You have only a week to study for this test. All essay questions. Be prepared to write." She smiles, straightens her papers, and heads for the door.

"I have another question," Franco says to Laura. "Are we going to pass this class?" She knows he is half serious, but Laura is worried about that, too.

Making sense of her notes may be only part of the challenge, but it is the first one she will have to overcome.

In This Chapter

Learning to listen and take notes effectively can give you the edge in college because you will be able to take in more information and remember it more easily. Laura can attest to the importance of developing a note-taking system, especially for those who have learning difficulties that prevent them from using just one style. This chapter discusses various note-taking strategies, including the method Laura developed, as well as improving your listening skills. When you complete this chapter, you will be able to:

* Describe ways to listen more effectively.
* Identify barriers to listening.
* Discuss different note-taking strategies.

The Listening and Note-Taking Connection

Listening, remembering, and note taking all have something in common: They are necessary in the process of learning. You will not be able to make it successfully through your classes without doing all three. Retaining and recalling information, however, is only part of the process. This chapter helps you with receiving the information, which will in turn help you with the process of turning the information into a knowledge base that you will build on for the rest of your life.

Preparing to Listen

Active listening is a term that you may hear in college classes; someone who listens actively is concentrating on what is being said and is taking steps to remember the information. The following tips are intended for those who want to listen actively and effectively. To be an active listener, you must decide that listening is a worthwhile activity and that important information will be shared.

The first step to effective listening is to prepare to listen before you get to class. In other words, you will need to read the assigned pages or chapters ahead of time so that you know what the lecture or discussion topic will be. If you have read the chapters ahead of time, you will be familiar with new words and concepts. Preparing to listen also includes reviewing your assigned readings before you get to the classroom. If you have a few minutes between classes or on the bus, pull out your book and skim the major headings, boldfaced terms, and text boxes that appear in the margins.

To listen effectively while in class, avoid distractions. First, you will need to sit up front, move away from a talkative person, and put away textbooks for other courses, cell phones, pagers, and other distracting items. Your best defense against interruptions is to clear your desk of anything except your textbook, a pen, and paper. Stow other items in your backpack or underneath your desk or table.

If you need to get anything out during class, such as a dictionary, minimize the disruption by being as quiet as possible. If you find yourself next to a chatty classmate or one who likes to write notes to you, simply move. Even if you are politely listening or reading her messages, you will be guilty of disrupting the class by association. Talkative classmates make it difficult for you and others to listen, and they distract you from taking good notes.

Another good way to listen effectively is by maintaining a positive attitude about the class. If you think the class is a waste of time or is boring, you will be less likely to pay attention. Even if your beliefs are true—and others bemoan the class as well—pretend that the class is the only one you have left before graduating and that if you don't pay attention and take good notes, then you will have to spend another semester in the course. In other words, do whatever you need to "psych" yourself up and invest in the class.

Minimizing outside distractions is another method of keeping a positive attitude. There will be times that you have to work late, stay up all night with a sick baby, or help a friend who has just had a crisis. If not handled well, these stressful experiences could affect your performance in class. As much as possible, leave your personal life at the door and concentrate on the class that you are sitting in. Even if the lecture for the day is overshadowed by a personal problem, remember that you *can* handle both your academic duties and your personal life.

Someone who listens actively is concentrating on what is being said and is taking steps to remember the information.

Finally, prepare for class psychologically by preparing physically. Make sure you have eaten something before each class so that you won't be interrupted by a growling stomach. Moreover, dress in layers in case the room is an uncomfortable temperature. Nothing is more distracting than being too hot or too cold. Getting plenty of sleep the night before class will also help you pay attention and listen effectively. Although adequate sleep may be a luxury if you work a late shift or if you get up in the middle of the night to take care of a child, be sure you make an effort to get a good night's sleep often. You won't be able to maintain high concentration and retention or even good health without adequate rest.

Listening Critically

As stated above, active listening, much like active reading, involves focusing on the task at hand and concentrating on what is being conveyed, whether it be words or sounds. Another part of listening effectively is listening critically, or the act of processing what you have heard and evaluating it. Listening critically will help you make decisions about what is important and what is not, what is objective and what is biased, and what should be stored for later and what should be discarded.

Listening critically is a skill, one that should be practiced regularly. Your college professors will invite you to think critically and challenge your assumptions (that is learning!). As you get more comfortable with listening actively and critically, you will move from merely listening and taking notes that reflect what your instructors have said to listening to evaluate and ask questions of the notes you have taken. Here are some questions to consider as you work on listening critically:

* *Speaker.* Is the speaker a credible source? How do I know? What possible biases does he or she have? What is his or her experience with the topic?

* *Message.* What is the speaker's purpose? What are the details he or she uses to convey the message?

* *Details.* Is the speaker using facts or opinions? How do I know? Which type of details work best for what the speaker is trying to convey?

* *Self-knowledge.* What do I already know about the topic? How does what the speaker is saying conflict or support my beliefs and opinions? Do I feel I have learned something new?

* *Larger picture.* How does what the speaker is saying fit into the larger picture? How can I relate the message to something I already know about life or the world at large? Are there any connections between what I have heard and what I have experienced?

Answering some of the questions above will get you started on the right path to listening critically. Even though you are listening critically and mentally asking questions of what you are hearing, you still need to "tune in" rather than "tune out" when you hear something that you don't agree with or don't understand.

Remember, too, that "critical" does not mean "negative." If you find that what you are hearing is not holding up to what you know about the subject or the speaker is not credible, you can still ask questions that are respectful and curious. Most people do not mind being politely challenged or debated.

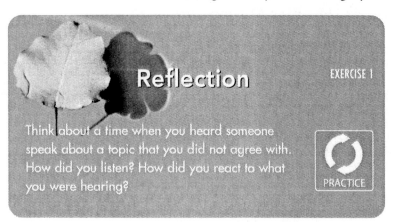

Reflection

EXERCISE 1

Think about a time when you heard someone speak about a topic that you did not agree with. How did you listen? How did you react to what you were hearing?

PRACTICE

Listening Barriers

Despite your efforts to prepare for class, you may find barriers to listening effectively, barriers that you cannot avoid no matter how well prepared you are. For example, what should you do if your instructor talks too fast, uses technical jargon or an advanced vocabulary, is unorganized, digresses from the lecture material (tells stories, allows too many irrelevant questions), or does not explain key concepts? Although you cannot coach your instructor in the art of speaking, you can ask him or her to slow down or define terms. Most professors do not mind repeating information or defining specialized language on the board because they want students to understand the material during lecture or class discussion.

It may be a little harder to ask the instructor to be more organized or to stay on topic during a lecture. However, one way to get what you need without offending the professor is to ask if she would mind providing an outline before each class. Another method of getting the professor to stay on the subject is to ask a question about the topic or an upcoming exam or assignment. Your nudging may move the lecture back into focus.

Besides getting enough sleep and sitting comfortably in class as discussed in the paragraphs above, there may be other barriers to listening effectively. If you have an unaccommodated learning disability or a hearing problem, you may not be able to listen productively. Talking to a counselor about learning or hearing difficulties can help you listen more effectively. A more common hindrance to listening is students' insecurities about their ability to do well in the course. It is not uncommon for a new student to feel, at first, intimidated by the course, the instructor, or other students in the class. The reason for the discomfort could stem from a student's feelings that he or she is not good enough or smart enough to be in college. A student also may feel that everyone else, except him or her, knows what to do, what to say, and how to act. This fear is common, and usually it subsides after the first week or two.

Remembering What You Have Heard

Once you adequately prepare to listen in class and you remove any barriers that inhibit your ability to take in information, you will need to turn your attention to remembering what you hear in class. Taking notes, of course, is one way to retain information. However, there are some other methods that will help you recall information at a later date.

Participating in discussion and activities is an excellent way to remember key concepts. In fact, professors consider student participation as part of active, rather than passive, learning. You are more likely to remember a concept if you have incorporated it into your own thinking. There is a reason that the most talkative students are usually the most successful. They have made the material relevant to them, which makes remembering easier for them as well. However, participating in class discussion may be difficult if you are shy or feel out of place in the classroom. Some students refrain from asking questions because they don't want to look ignorant in front of their classmates.

Then, there is the other end of the spectrum from the silent student—the constant questioner. These students dominate the professor's time by asking questions that sideline the discussion or questions about material that has already been covered. Don't be intimidated by a predominantly quiet classroom or by a student who asks the professor excessive questions. If you have a question, ask it. Some instructors believe there are no "stupid questions." If you don't feel comfortable asking questions during class, visit with your professor after class or during his office hours. Some instructors ask students to write questions down and pass them up before class is over. Take advantage of such a practice; you will be able to ask questions without the fear of speaking up in front of classmates.

Another method for remembering, tape recording lectures, is popular with students who have the time to listen. Listening to a tape recording will work best if you have a long commute or if you go over your notes as you listen. Be sure to ask permission before you turn the tape recorder on, and make sure you have fresh batteries with you in case they run down.

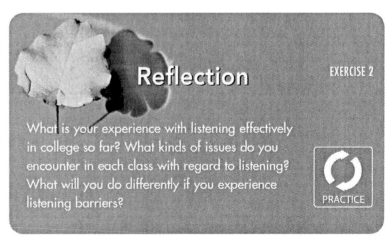

Reflection
EXERCISE 2

What is your experience with listening effectively in college so far? What kinds of issues do you encounter in each class with regard to listening? What will you do differently if you experience listening barriers?

PRACTICE

INTEGRITY MATTERS

Listening with integrity means that you listen with an open mind and without judgment until the speaker is finished. Then, you can ask questions of the speaker if there are points that you don't understand. Listening with integrity also means that you avoid twisting the person's words to fit what you want to hear. Practicing active and critical listening will help you maintain integrity.

How Information Is Presented

Learning to listen effectively is the first step to taking good notes, but you will also benefit from understanding how information can be presented during a lecture. As you attend more classes, you will probably notice that professors have a certain way in which they present their material. Some will follow the textbook information in the same order. Others will lecture only on new material that cannot be found in the textbook or other course materials. Then, others will present a combination of the two methods. Reading assigned chapters and materials before you attend class will allow you to determine which information in the lecture is new and which has been covered in assigned reading materials.

There are many different ways information can be organized. Recognizing the different ways material can be organized will help you stay organized in your notes and will provide you with strategies for revising and reviewing your notes when you begin studying.

* *Chronological*—details arranged in time (first this happened, then this happened, etc.).

   EXAMPLE OF CHRONOLOGICAL LECTURE NOTES

   1801: United Kingdom of Great Britain is created

   1803: Louisiana Purchase is made by Thomas Jefferson

   1815: Battle of Waterloo signals end of Napoleon's career

* *Cause/effect*—details arranged by presenting a cause and then its effects or an effect and its causes.

   EXAMPLE OF CAUSE/EFFECT LECTURE NOTES

   Cause: Civil War

   Effects: slavery ended, industrialism began, the nation was brought back together, the federal government proved stronger than the states

* *Compare/contrast*—details arranged by similarities and differences.

   EXAMPLE OF COMPARISON/CONTRAST LECTURE NOTES

   Similarities between Robert Frost and Walt Whitman: they were males; they used nature in their poetry; and they were considered "poets of the people." Differences between Frost and Whitman: Frost's poetry is more structured, while Whitman's is open and loose; Whitman's speakers are more positive and upbeat than Frost's; Whitman lived during the 19th century while Frost lived in both the 19th and 20th centuries.

* *Most important/least important*—details arranged in order of importance. The most important detail can come first with minor supporting details to follow, or the least important details can start a list that works to a major detail.

EXAMPLE OF MOST IMPORTANT/LEAST IMPORTANT LECTURE NOTES

Self-awareness (purpose of education)

Values

Goals

Mission

Personality type

Learning style

Note-Taking Strategies

There are numerous methods of taking notes for a class. Your goal should be to find the note-taking strategy that works best for you. Remember that you may have to adapt your note-taking style to each course, each teaching style, and each learning style strength. For example, outlining may work well in a history course in which the instructor writes key terms on the board and organizes her lecture around key ideas. If your professor prefers unstructured discussion, you will need to adapt your note-taking strategy to make the most of unorganized information.

Whatever you choose for the particular course, your learning style, and the specific situation, there are a few tips that you need to remember when taking notes.

* Listen for the main ideas.

Instructors will slow down and emphasize information, terms, and definitions. They may even use verbal signposts such as "The most important thing to remember is," "This may appear on an exam," or "Two crucial points about . . . ." If the instructor writes or hands out an outline, you can be sure that it contains the main points of the lecture.

* Leave plenty of "white space" (blank space on paper) when taking notes.

Don't try to fill your page with as much information as possible. You will need the white space to add more notes or to synthesize ideas once you have reviewed.

* Review your notes as soon as possible after class.

Waiting for two weeks to review your notes will ensure that you won't remember everything that you have written or how it all fits together. Most experts suggest that you review your notes within two days of the class.

Developing a Shorthand

As you take more notes in each class, you will find yourself using a few of the same words over and over again. These words are good candidates for abbreviating or denoting in symbols. You can then create your own shorthand. Shortened words such as "ex." for "example," "w/" for "with," and "b/c" for "because" are abbreviations you probably already use in notes and email messages. Symbols that you may already use include % for "percentage," + for "add" or "and," and # for "number." If you use a new abbreviation or symbol for a word, be sure to make a note of what it means; for example, "TR" could mean "Theory of Relativity" in a science course and "Teddy Roosevelt" in a history course.

Here is a list of other commonly abbreviated words and symbols:

At	@
Between	betw, b/w
Decrease	decr
Department	dept
Does not equal	≠
Government	govt
Increase	incr
Equals	=
Example	eg, ex
Important	imp
Information	info
Regarding	re
Significant	sig

Developing a shorthand will allow you more time to concentrate on what is being said. As you get more practice, you will become better at judging what information is worth writing and what is not, and your shorthand will become more efficient. Just remember to read over your notes within a day or two so that your abbreviations are fresh in your mind. It is a good idea, then, to complete the words or concepts so that you won't struggle to remember what all the shortened words mean later in the semester. Plus, it will reinforce your learning the material.

Outlining

Using an outline is a good method for taking notes if the instructor is organized and offers information in a logical pattern. Some instructors encourage outlining by writing key words and concepts on the board or an overhead projecting device. If your instructor organizes lectures or class discussions in that manner, you will be able to write an outline for your notes quite easily. The key to making your outlines effective will be to provide plenty of space between the items so that you can fill in the blank spaces with extra information. An example of an outline for a lecture on effective listening could look like this:

I. Preparing to Listen Effectively

II. Listening Critically

III. Possible Listening Barriers

    A. External

        1. Hunger

        2. Climate discomfort

    B. Internal

        1. Feelings of self-worth

        2. Stress

IV. How Information Is Presented

    A. Chronological

    B. Cause/Effect

    C. Compare/Contrast

    D. Most Important/Least Important

Taking Notes within the Textbook

Writing in the margins of your textbook can be another effective way to take notes, especially if the reading assignment is lengthy. If you don't mind writing directly in your textbook, you can summarize main points that you have read. Writing brief summaries (two- or three-word summaries) or questions in the margins will help you make sense of and remember what you have read. Brief, marginal summaries will also help you review the material before class and after class when you start studying for an exam.

Annotating in your textbook and writing down critical questions are two methods of further reinforcing what you have read and will help you prepare for listening and note taking in class. To write critical questions about the reading, ask questions such as "How do I know this to be true?" and "What else should be considered?" Annotating your textbook with your own notes will help you not only reinforce main ideas, but will also help you synthesize the information in new ways that will produce connections between concepts, making the material more memorable and more relevant.

If you decide to write in the margins of your textbook, be sure that the book you are writing in is not one that you want to sell back to the bookstore. If you do not want to write in your book but still get the benefits of summarizing the material, you can write your summaries on a separate sheet of paper. Make sure that you label each piece of paper with the chapter title and page number of the book.

Highlighting in your textbook is another method that students use for taking notes on reading material. A highlighter pen can be used to mark important concepts for review, but be careful that you do not highlight too much information. Over-highlighting the text can have the opposite effect—instead of making it easier to understand key terms and information, too much highlighting can make everything seem of equal importance. If you do use a highlighter pen, use it sparingly. For example, don't highlight more than two sentences in a row. A better method would be to use highlighting and written summaries together for the greatest effect.

The Cornell System

Cornell University professor Dr. Walter Pauk developed a system for note taking that has been popular with many students. The Cornell System, also known as the T System, is ideal for those who benefit from the visual impact of organized notes, and it can benefit other types of learners, such as Laura, because it is an organized way to take and review notes. The key to the Cornell System is dividing your notebook paper before you begin writing. To do so, you draw a horizontal line across your piece of paper two inches from the bottom of the page. Then, you draw a vertical line from the horizontal line to the top of the page about 2 inches from the lefthand margin. The page should look like Figure 1.

The largest area, the righthand column, is used for taking notes during class. The lefthand column is used for asking questions as you take notes if there is material you don't understand during the lecture or if there are possible exam questions that you think about as you are writing. At the bottom, the final section is reserved for summarizing your notes as you review them. The act of summarizing should help you understand and remember the information.

Critical Thinking

EXERCISE 3

What are some drawbacks to using the Cornell System, shorthand, and outlines when taking notes?

PRACTICE

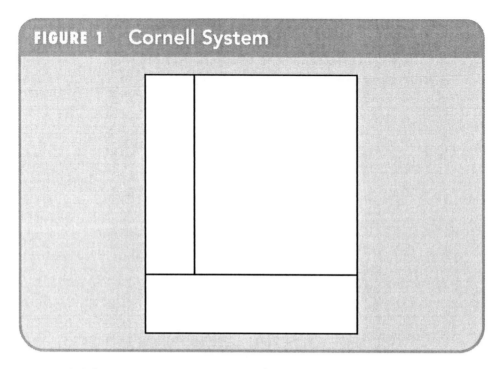

FIGURE 1   Cornell System

Note-Taking Strategies in the Disciplines

The following strategies for note taking in the disciplines are just a sample of what you may encounter in college. Specific study strategies differ within disciplines, but here we give some note-taking strategies, grouped by discipline, that will make reviewing your notes and studying easier.

Art. In an art appreciation class, you will need to identify eras (20th century), movements (Cubism), and artists (Picasso) as well as their characteristics, as seen in drawings, paintings, and sculpture. Quickly sketching the works in your notes and listing the characteristic details will help you record the information you are receiving through lectures. You may also notice that in the study of art there are times of intense change (usually coinciding with a world or cultural event) followed by artists who imitate or modify slightly the new style. As you review your notes, look for patterns within groups of artwork and for points of contrast.

Music. In a music appreciation class, the same suggestions for an art appreciation class will work when you take notes. Instead of recreating a painting or sculpture in your notes, you may need to write down descriptions of what you are hearing and what the sounds remind you of. Are the sounds fast or slow? Do you hear one instrument or many? Does it sound like a stampede or a trip down a lazy river? "Translating" music samples into written notes as well as reviewing music clips on your own will strengthen your understanding of the material. As with your art notes, upon review, look for patterns across movements and eras and denote contrasting ideas and elements.

Literature. Taking notes in a literature class will require that you have completed the assigned readings before class and that you have annotated and highlighted your text. Because literature classes, even survey classes, focus more on discussion than on lecture, you will want to be prepared to take notes on the analysis. As with music and art classes, being familiar with basic terminology before you get to class will help you take better notes. As you review your notes, look for ideas that pull the different readings together.

Languages. Foreign language classes center more on speaking and interacting than on listening to a lecture. Taking notes will not necessarily be advantageous, for you will need to focus all your attention on listening actively, processing what is heard, and interacting based on what you have heard. Daily preparation is essential to learning foreign languages; take notes as you encounter new material, and ask questions in class to get clarification on anything you do not understand. Any notes you do take should be reviewed soon after the class. As you review your notes, categorize material such as "irregular verbs" and include any tips for using or remembering the parts of language.

Science. Concepts and processes are key in science classes and your notes will reflect that. Prepare for class by reading assigned material, making note of new vocabulary words, and studying diagrams and figures in the text and handouts. As with any class, ask questions if you are having trouble following the steps of a process. As you review your notes, consider the different ways that you can represent these concepts and processes visually and physically.

History. History class lectures are usually presented in chronological order, so using the tips above for information that follows a time sequence will help you take notes in this class. However, you will also be required to move beyond specific dates and events by considering overall themes, ideas, and movements. In addition to chronological order, lectures may also use a cause/effect organization in which you list and elaborate on the effects of a cause or the causes of an effect. An example of a lecture topic in a history class is "The economic and social effects of the end of the Civil War." As you review your notes, look for major themes and be able to recall actions that have led to important events.

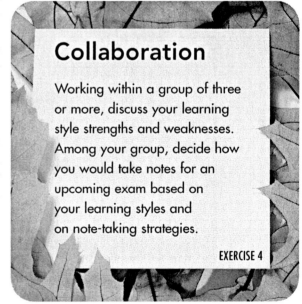

Collaboration

Working within a group of three or more, discuss your learning style strengths and weaknesses. Among your group, decide how you would take notes for an upcoming exam based on your learning styles and on note-taking strategies.

EXERCISE 4

Math. Taking good notes in your math classes will require that you prepare and attend each class meeting. As with foreign languages, studying for math should be an everyday occurrence because the skills you learn in each class build on the ones you learned in the class before. When reviewing your notes, you may want to recopy them and make sure that you understand, line by line of each problem, what you are copying. If you have any questions, you can write them in the margins of your notes and ask questions during the next class meeting.

Finding Your Own Note-Taking Style

Laura has developed a special note-taking system for herself because of a learning disability. After taking an introduction to college course, she discovered that the note-taking systems that were discussed in her textbook did not help her take good notes. Through trial and error, she developed a system that works for her.

To begin with, Laura writes in pencil on her notebook paper. Before class begins, she dates each page and leaves herself plenty of room to write. When taking notes, she writes on only one side of the page; in fact, most of her pages of notes contain less than fifty words. While she uses more pieces of paper, her notes are easier to read.

EXHIBIT 1   Laura's Notes

Ancient   (1st)   Jehovah
                  Jewish Beliefs—Monotheism

Jews divided	all humanity
Strictly-segregated	
We (Jews)	They (Gentiles) ✡
No outside conversion	non-Jewish
convenant with God	place on earth
↓	↓
chosen people	Tempters & obstacles
family-most important	
↓	Sacred text
society revolved around	Old Testament
Patriarchal male-dominant	
↓	Jehovah (Yahweh)
more rights	share-Christianity concepts (similar)
⊕ marriage-lineage	① Fall of man from grace
⊖ bachelor-frowned	② Day of judgment
male married by 24	③ Immortality
prefer 20	④ 1 God (worship)
Female-13 can marry	
↓	
more children	

Next, she stars words that the instructor says are important. The most important part of her note-taking system is her use of arrows to make connections between ideas. By giving herself plenty of room, she can add connections that are revealed later in the lecture. If her instructor reviews the material before an exam, Laura highlights what she already has and adds notes in the spaces.

One strategy that Laura has developed to help her with her learning disability is that she doesn't worry about spelling. To make connections between ideas, she draws lines between words that relate to each other. She also makes charts for anything that is compared and contrasted (see Laura's notes in the accompanying figure). Finally, she keeps all of her notes in a binder that is divided for each class. Staying organized is an important part of her method. Although she uses only one binder during the semester, she keeps her notes easily organized by removing them after an exam. When she takes out notes she no longer needs, she places them in labeled folders at home. Then she carries with her only the notes she needs at that time.

A Note on Note-Takers

There may be a time that you will rely on someone to take notes for you while you are absent, or you may have a learning or physical disability that allows you to ask someone in the class to take notes for you all semester. Student or professional note-takers provide an important service for disabled students or unique learners so they can receive the same educational opportunities as other students. Whether or not you depend on someone every once in a while or for the duration of your education, there are still things you should consider:

* If possible, review the note-taker's notes with the note-taker or others in the class. Because the physical act of taking notes helps students remember the information, you will need to find other ways to reinforce the material.
* Stay focused when you are in class. Find ways to help you remember the material as well, such as creating visual maps or scenes in your mind.
* Prepare for class beforehand. Since you won't be taking notes, your preparation is critical.
* Don't take your note-taker for granted by missing class or not preparing. The note-taker is not a surrogate student, but a supplement.
* If your note-taker's notes are difficult to read, incomplete, or missing because he does not attend regularly, talk to the disability services counselor. She can arrange for a new note-taker.

Reviewing Your Notes

Notes are only as good as the extent to which that you review them. If you never looked at your notes after you took them, they would serve very little purpose. Therefore, to make the most of your notes, you will need to review them. As stated earlier in the chapter, reviewing should be done within two days from the time you took them. With this said, it is easy to be lulled into the sense of "studying" by merely reading over your notes again and again. When reviewing your notes, it is best to reorganize the material, make connections between concepts—even across disciplines—and ask questions about what you are learning.

If you use the Cornell System, then you have a built-in area for adding more information, summarizing, and asking yourself questions. However, if you do not use a particular method, you can still benefit from filling in any blanks or holes in your notes with information you have since learned. As stated earlier, you should also spell out any abbreviations you have that may cause confusion later. After you fill in any gaps, you should also include questions—either on the same page or a new page— that will help you think about the material on a deeper level. For example, asking "Why is it important to know this?" can help you move beyond demonstrating your comprehension of the material to making it relevant and useful for you.

Freewriting about the material that you learned is another way of remembering and learning the information that you have listened to. This technique is often used as a way to generate ideas for writing, but it can also be used to take advantage of all the thoughts you have in your head about the material. For optimum effectiveness, you will need to freewrite within a day or two of the class lecture. With or without your notes, write down (or type into a word processor) all the information that you remember from the class.

The key to freewriting is continuation; in other words, do not stop writing even if you can't spell a certain word or get stuck on a particular idea. Give yourself 5 or 10 minutes to freewrite; then, go through your freewriting material (some of it you will be able to use and some of it you will scratch out) and highlight or rewrite into complete sentences the information that pertains to the lecture. In essence, you will be learning the material in more depth as you write about it.

Finally, reciting notes with a friend can be a useful method for reviewing material. You can do this in person or on the phone. The benefits of reading your notes aloud and discussing them include filling in any gaps of information and reinforcing what you have learned. You can also engage in critical questioning of the material and take turns making connections between major concepts.

TIPS FOR SUCCESSFUL NOTE-TAKING

* Prepare for class by reading *all* the assigned material before arriving. If you cannot read all of it, then read as much as you can.
* Prepare to listen actively by removing distractions and bringing supplies.
* Listen actively; concentrate on what you are hearing, seeing, and experiencing.
* Listen critically by asking questions, either on paper or directly in class if your professor encourages questions during class.
* Use a note-taking strategy that takes into account both your learning style strength and the subject matter.
* Go beyond reviewing your notes by only rereading them; instead, focus on concepts and main ideas, make connections between the large ideas, and ask critical questions of processes and ideas.
* Continue the process regularly throughout the semester.

PLUS

(Personality + Learning Style = Understanding Situations)

EXERCISE 5

Think about Laura's note-taking situation in her history class. Because Laura is an introverted person, she finds it hard to ask questions in class or visit her professor one-on-one to get help; she is more comfortable with her mentor or the tutors on campus and is willing to get help from them. Because she has dyslexia, she is very motivated and works hard in her classes, often reviewing and rewriting her notes several times when she studies. However, the variety of ways she needs to arrange and remember information for this class is a challenge. Using what you have learned from this chapter, what advice would you give her? How can she make the most of her note-taking situation and learn the material with confidence?

Now, considering your own learning style, personality type, and special circumstances, what would you do to take notes in a class that requires a variety of ways to organize the material?

PROFILE

MY STORY
Learning Plan

Directions: Using what you have learned in this chapter and what you know about your learning preferences, choose a task or assignment that needs to be completed soon and create a learning plan that will help you accomplish this task. Then, write your *My Story* Summary, a one-sentence synopsis that crystallizes your newly created plan.

LEARNING TASK	
Time of Day	
Intake Preference	
Social Preference	
Task Management Preference	

MY STORY SUMMARY:

Path of Discovery

Journal Entry

Have you ever experienced a time in which you did not listen? What happened and what did you learn from the experience?

HOMEWORK

From College to University

Improving Listening and Note-Taking Skills When There Are More Distractions

When you transfer to a four-year university, the good habits that you have practiced at your community college will help you succeed. However, you may find that you have more distractions. There may be more people on campus and in your classes, more organizations and associations to join, more activities to participate in, and more stress in deciding on a major and getting ready to graduate.

In addition to distractions, you may also find that professors at four-year universities lecture less and rely more on student discussion and presentations. Your ability to organize the material into coherent parts will be vitally important to your making sense of the course. If you find yourself at a loss for what to do to take good notes, talk to others who have been at the university longer than you. They may have their own tips. It may also be a good idea, now more than ever, to join a study group or at least find a "study buddy" to review your notes with. While you may have done well studying by yourself at the community college, you may now realize that group interaction and work is not only encouraged but also necessary for success.

From College to Career

Practicing Critical Listening Skills Will Give You an Edge on the Job

Most of the communication you will do on the job will involve listening: listening to clients' urgent needs, your employer's plans for the next six months, coworkers' explanations of how they would complete a project, and subordinates' questions about how to improve. Being a good listener will involve practicing the critical listening tips that are outlined in this chapter. Why do you need to listen critically on the job? The reason for cultivating this skill is that you will be bombarded with information at all levels: above you from your boss, at the same level as you from your coworkers, and below you from those who work for you. Critical listening skills will enable you to filter what you are hearing so that you can act appropriately and avoid making errors in action and judgment. Consider, for example, a coworker who comes to you to complain about a company policy. Without listening actively and critically, you may disregard what the speaker is saying because you don't have time to do anything about it. However, if you took the time to analyze the speaker (Is she a credible source?) and the message (Is the purpose to vent or to change something?) as well as what you know about the situation yourself (Is the policy flawed and in need of change?) and the larger picture (How will this proposed change affect others?), then you are more likely to act appropriately and confidently. On the job, as in life, you will not—and should not—respond the same to all messages you receive from speakers. Practicing critical listening skills will make it easier to determine which messages are critical and which can be acted upon later—which will make you a more efficient and effective employee.

Chapter Review Questions

1. What is the difference between active and critical listening?
2. What are the potential listening barriers in the classroom?
3. In what ways can information be presented in class?
4. List and describe the different note-taking strategies.
5. Name three disciplines and describe how note-taking differs in each.

Case Scenarios

1. Juan is taking a visual arts class and is having trouble making sense of his notes each week because they are over information that pertains to specific artwork. The instructor does not hand out reproductions of the art, so the student must sketch the pieces during class, but that takes too long. Do you have any other suggestions for Juan besides trying to draw the actual artwork?

2. Theo has borrowed Jon's notes for his College Algebra class and has promised to return them before the next exam. However, Theo has lost them, and with only two days left before the next test, he is not sure what to do. Jon is a good student and probably doesn't need them as much as he, but he wants to be able to borrow future notes from Jon. What should he do?

3. Karla has a learning difficulty, and she struggles with taking notes. The counselor has assigned her a note-taker. Now that Karla is getting help with writing down notes, she has stopped preparing for class and has stopped listening closely. Sometimes, she doesn't get notes from her note-taker until a week later. If you were Karla's friend or counselor, what advice would you give her about using a note-taker?

Research It Further

1. Take a survey of the students in one of your other classes as to which of the discussed note-taking strategies they use the most. Create a table of your results and present them to your classmates.

2. Using the key words "note-taking strategies," search the Internet for websites that offer note-taking methods. Choose two or three and review the information to determine which site offers the most practical and complete tips. Present your findings to the class.

3. Create your own note-taking or listening strategy and present it to the class, highlighting the benefits of your method over another method.

Studying and Taking Tests

4

From Chapter 10 of *The Community College Experience Plus,* Second Edition, Amy Baldwin.

Studying and Taking Tests

Four Students' Stories

Studying the origins of life in their Biology 101 class is becoming an exercise in their own survival. Juanita, Evan, Michael, and Laura formed a study group early in the semester, on the suggestion of their orientation leaders, and now it has become a precious lifeline. Their professor is great, they all agree, but the mountain of chapters, notes, extra readings, papers, and lab work is killing them.

"So much work for just one class," Michael says. "It's insane."

"Ha," Juanita replies, "I'm taking world literature and psychology. The reading alone takes me hours each night."

Both Michael and Juanita got to their study group early so that they could get a good booth in the food court before it gets crowded. Nervous about the first test, Michael thinks he has studied too much of the wrong things. Juanita has severe test anxiety anytime she takes a test, and studying with a group helps her relax before the big day.

"Are you starting without me?" Laura asks as she drops her heavy backpack on the booth seat by Michael.

"Of course not," Juanita says. "Michael was just crying about how much work this class is. I had to remind him of my schedule—nonstop reading that will make your eyes cross."

"My mother finished her degree right before I started school and I remember how much she studied. If she can do it, I think I can," Laura says. "But I am *not* ready for this test. Between a sick kid and a paper for history, I couldn't fit it in."

"Does anyone know what the test will cover? I think I have studied all the wrong material," Michael says.

"I have to study everything, even if I don't think it will be on the test," says Juanita. "If I'm not overprepared, I know I will lose it when I get the test. I've been studying since the first week of classes."

"Why am I not surprised?" Evan asks as he slides into a seat next to Michael. "Sorry, I'm late. I had to run by the gym. What have I missed besides Juanita reciting every biology fact from the first day of class?"

The study group laughs at Evan's comment, but they know he usually gets by with little studying. When he does meet with his group, he comes late or leaves early and rarely brings his notes or book.

"Can we get serious now? I have to pass this test," Laura says. Her single parent scholarship requires that she maintain a 3.0 GPA, and Laura works hard to keep it.

"I suggest we start going over everything that we have done since the first chapter," Juanita suggests. "If we work on this for the next four hours, then we can study four more tomorrow. I will probably stay up late tomorrow night to make sure I get it."

Evan, text-messaging while he talks, says, "If we just review our notes, we should be fine. When was the last time you failed a test? They have to give you something for just taking it."

"If I don't know it now, I won't know it in two days and that really scares me," says Laura.

Michael chews on the end of his pen and checks his watch. "I don't have much time to study tonight. My girlfriend needs a ride to work," he says.

"We need to start somewhere even if we can't all stay the whole time or agree on how to do this," says the youngest of the group who has stepped up as the leader.

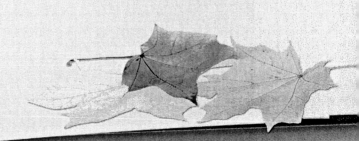

In This Chapter

As they discuss in their study group, Juanita, Michael, Evan, and Laura have various levels of preparation for their upcoming biology test and different perspectives on how they should study over the next two days. Just as Laura admits to the group and Evan demonstrates by his late arrival, you may also have competing priorities and tasks that keep you from studying, or you may feel anxious about taking the test as Michael and Juanita reveal.

Whatever your experience with studying is until this point in your academic career, professors and experienced students alike agree that good preparation will make studying much easier. In fact, you may learn to look forward to studying, especially as you take classes that interest you and that apply to your career. This chapter's purpose is to help you improve your study skills, which will in turn help you improve your test-taking strategies. No matter what you have heard, successful students study frequently and effectively. If you have never been "good at" studying, you can improve your skills by following the steps that work best for you.

This chapter provides you with study strategies for preparing for tests effectively as well as tips for taking a test to maximize your success. Specifically, at the end of this chapter you will be able to:

* Determine the best study strategies.

* Identify strategies for effective study groups.

* Describe the kinds of test questions you will encounter and how best to answer them.

* List methods for reducing test anxiety.

Testing, 1, 2, 3

Although the terms are usually used interchangeably, a *test* is defined as a set of questions that are used to evaluate one's skills, aptitudes, and abilities on certain topics. Usually, tests assess your knowledge and abilities on a part of the course. An *exam*, however, by definition is an assessment of the material of an entire course. Final exams are sometimes called *comprehensive* or *cumulative* exams, which indicate that they will cover what you have studied all semester or term.

Unless your professor tells you directly what will be on the test, assume that anything that was assigned or covered in class may be there. Just about every college student has a story about taking a test that covered reading assignments and not what was discussed in class. These students were surprised to realize that studying the lecture notes was not enough. The following is a list of items that you may be tested on for any class:

* Material from the lecture, discussion, and in-class or out-of-class activity

* Information provided by a guest speaker

* Information from a workshop or field trip

* Multimedia productions such as video or audio

* Assigned readings, including chapters in the textbook

* Handouts including PowerPoint slides and outlines

You can be assured that you will encounter a variety of test types. Take clues from what you do in class to help determine what kind of test questions you may encounter. For example, if your professor spends time applying information from a chapter during class or as an assignment, then you will likely have test questions that will ask you to apply the information as well. Listen for clues that the professor gives you, such as "You should write this down" and "This is a really important point." Other cue phrases include "You may see this again on a test" and "If you saw this on a test, how would you answer it?" When you hear these phrases, write them down and review them when studying over your other notes. A professor who says these things is begging you to take notice!

The best advice to give college students is plain and simple: Study for all tests. No exceptions. Sometimes you will find that you do not need to study as much for some classes; however, remember that studying effectively is a habit. To form the long-term habit, you must do it even when you don't think you have to, which is fundamental to making an activity part of a routine, something Evan may need help establishing for himself.

A Place and Time for Studying

The best time to begin studying is as soon as the semester starts. Be careful of the mindset that because you are not in class every day you don't need to study every day. Some students begin studying the night or day before an exam, which may be too late to review and remember all the material that has been covered over the past several weeks. Start reviewing your notes within two days of taking them. If possible, you should start studying for future exams right now, today.

If you are a typical college student, then your time will be limited. You may not have the luxury of large blocks of time, so you will need to be creative about studying. Because it is more effective to study for short periods of time, consider studying in between classes, during breaks at work, and on the way to work and school (provided you are not driving). Another way to ensure that you study during the day is to get in the habit of always carrying your notes or books with you—this way you'll be able to take advantage of any unexpected "free" time. You can also get up earlier or stay up later so you can spend a few minutes studying before starting or ending your day.

If you have the luxury of choosing when to study, rather than sandwiching it in between work and family responsibilities, pay attention to what *time of day* you are most alert and receptive to learning. The best time of day for you to study is dependent on your schedule, your responsibilities, your age, and your personal preferences. Some people identify themselves as "night owls" whereas others claim to be "morning people." Whatever your peak performance time, be sure to study your most difficult subjects at that time. If you have a predictable schedule all semester, plan to study at the same time each day.

The environment in which you study is just as important as the time of day and the length of time you spend studying. You will need to find the kind of environment that works well for you. Some people need complete silence with no visual distractions, whereas others need a little background noise to stay focused. At the least, create a place that is comfortable, has good lighting, and has space for your supplies and books. It is easier to make time to study when you have a place to do it. If you have nowhere at home that is quiet and roomy, then search for a place on campus or a local library that offers study space. Some people find that studying away from home is better because they are not distracted by the television, phone, or family members.

Small children can pose a particular difficulty in finding quiet time. If you have small children, make a concerted effort to find a quiet spot. You may need to hire a baby-sitter or find a classmate who can trade child care services with you when you want to study. For example, you could offer to baby-sit a classmate's kids when he needs to study in exchange for him watching yours when you have a paper to write. Some college students who are also parents find time to study only when their children are asleep. Therefore, their best studying takes place late at night or early in the morning at home. Do whatever works best for you.

How to Study Effectively

Setting Goals

Once you have determined when, where, and how much you need to study, set study and test-taking goals. Write down goals that you want to achieve when studying and taking tests. Remember the title of Henriette Anne Klauser's book: *Write It Down, Make It Happen* (2001). This also applies to something as short term as studying for and taking a test. Your goals could be as simple as the following:

- *I will use my time wisely so that I am able to study all my notes.*
- *I will ask the instructor questions about any notes that I do not understand.*
- *I will remain calm before, during, and after the exam by practicing breathing techniques and by relaxing.*

Of course, your goals could also include studying with a group or making a high grade. If you have never written down goals for studying or taking tests, then start small. Once you have achieved your study and test-taking goals, create newer and more challenging ones with each test:

- *I will improve my writing skills by practicing the essay questions in a timed environment.*
- *I will improve my overall retention of the material after the test.*

Studying Actively

Goal setting is just one of the ways to prepare for exams, but one of the most important is how you approach studying. In order to build a body of knowledge, you will want to study to *learn*, not just to *remember*. In other words, you will want to transfer information from your short-term memory, which holds information for a short period of time, to your long-term memory, which can be retrieved long after it is "deposited" there.

One of the ways to improve your memory of the material you have learned is to actively take it in when you study. The goal of active studying is to make connections between concepts and theories so that you can more easily recall the information and write or speak knowledgeably about it. To achieve this kind of mastery, instead of simply rereading notes or passively reviewing the major headings in your textbook, your studying should include activities such as the following:

- Rewriting or summarizing your notes.
- Rearranging the order of the material from most important to least important detail; from least important to most important; or in chronological order.

* Making connections between what you have learned in one chapter, unit, or class with material you have learned in other places.
* Making connections between what you have learned in class and what you have experienced in the real world.
* Explaining concepts to someone else who is not familiar with the topic.
* Making visual representations of the material.

Creating a Study Log

After considering your study goals, you may also want to create a study log that will help you keep track of your tests and preparation steps. Figure 1 is an example of a study log.

Understanding Course Objectives

Another step in studying effectively is to understand the objectives of the course. You will find the course objectives in the syllabus or in other material that has been handed out to you in class. If one of your course objectives is to identify the processes of cell replication, then you can be sure that you will be tested on the processes of cell replication in some manner. Making sure that you study the material that appears in course objectives will help you focus your time and energy on the right course content.

Using Time Wisely

How much time you spend and how many sessions you have will depend on the type of learner you are. You could start with 45 minutes of studying three different times a day over the period of a week to see how well you retain and remember the material. Adjust your schedule as needed. Just remember to be conscious of how effective your study sessions are. If they are not helping you meet your study goals, then make changes in your schedule. In Evan's case, his biology study group may not be helping

FIGURE 1 Study Log	
Class	**Chemistry**
Date	Tuesday, October 27
Material	Chapters 4–7, extra lecture material
Practice/Previous Tests	In library on reserve; answer key for practice test
Question Types	Multiple choice, problem solving
Study Methods	Review notes, work through extra problems, go through practice test, study with group
Time Needed	6 hours
Approved Materials for Test	Paper, pencil, calculator
Number of Points	150, 15% of overall grade

him study in the manner that is most effective for him. If that is the case, he may need to find a different group that fits his study goals better or consider that studying alone is his best option.

No matter how much time you spend studying, it won't be effective if you are unable to concentrate on the subject. Many times you will find yourself distracted by external and internal commotion. Externally, you may have a noisy or messy house, or you may have others who need or want your time and attention. Internally, you may be preoccupied by illness, stress, self-doubt, or fear. Both internal and external distractions make it difficult to study effectively, so you must take care of them or tune them out. If not, you will find that the time you spend studying is not productive.

Reflection

What are your experiences with studying? When do you study and for how long? Has it been successful for you? Why or why not?

EXERCISE 1

PRACTICE

For some students, planning ahead to study effectively is not an option. Because of poor time management or procrastination, these students often try to study in one long session of cramming. Cramming and marathon sessions should be avoided when studying for an exam because they usually produce more anxiety than learning. If you do find yourself in a situation in which you must cram, try to maximize the effectiveness of the long hours and loads of material. Organize your time into short periods, no more than one hour at a time, and take many breaks. When you return from your break, review the material you had just been studying before you begin on new material. You may want to try a combination of writing down what you know, drawing pictures to represent the material, reciting key concepts aloud, creating songs with the material, or building a model of a key idea. The more learning preferences you use to understand the material, the better your chance of remembering it all for the test.

There is no reason that studying cannot include having fun. Some websites offer games and fun quizzes to help you study. One such site is www.quia.com. However, you don't have to look for games that are produced by others; you can create your own. Consider making flash cards to quiz yourself or others if you are in a study group. You can also tape-record questions and answers. Instead of playing the tape straight through, stop the tape after each question so you can answer the question aloud. Then, play the answer and see how well you have done. If you can push yourself to enjoy studying, you will be more likely to do it often.

"Cheat" Sheets

Creating "cheat" sheets was once considered an activity only for those who intended to cheat; however, many educators have seen the benefit that creating such sheets can have. You may have a professor who tells you that you can bring a three-by-five-inch index card to the exam with anything you want written on it. Students who may not have studied much beforehand usually jump at the chance to cram as much information as possible on that tiny, white space. The result is that students retain more of the information than they would if they had not created the cheat sheet. Many times, the cheat sheet is not needed because the student has, in effect, studied adequately in making the sheet.

To create an effective cheat sheet, organization is important. One way to organize the card is to divide it into thirds on both sides so that you have six sections (three on one side, three on the other) to work with. Then, use the top of each section to write a specific category such as "Formulas" or "Krebs Cycle." Underneath each heading, write the information that pertains to the category. If you are listing formulas, for example, be sure to write clearly and double check that all elements of the formula are correct.

Even if you are not allowed to bring a cheat sheet—only bring one if you are given permission—you can still reap the benefits of this technique by closing your books and notes and writing down as much information as you can remember about the subject. For example, if you have a test on genetics, take a blank card and write everything you know about DNA on the front and back. In this case, organization is not important; what is important is to see how much you have learned already. Once you have filled up the card, go back through your notes and books to see what you have missed.

Previous Exams and Practice Tests

If allowed by the instructor, study copies of old tests. Your instructor will put them on reserve in the library, post them online in an online learning system, or hand them out in class. Previous exams are an excellent source for what kinds of questions you will be asked. If someone offers to give you his old tests from the previous semester, ask your instructor first if you can study from them before taking them.

Equally beneficial to understanding how your professor will test you is to take advantage of practice exams if they are offered. Some instructors may provide opportunities for you to stop by during office hours to take a practice exam or to take an online practice test where you can get instant feedback.

Study Groups

Juanita, Michael, Laura, and Evan took the advice of their orientation leaders early in the semester to create a study group for one of their classes, and they have realized that there are several benefits of studying in groups. First, you have access to more notes and may find that you have missed important information. Second, you experience others' perspectives about the subject, and you may find that your classmates explain major concepts better than your professor. Third, you have a built-in support group while you take classes, because in the process of studying, you establish friendships.

A key to a successful study group is to limit the group to four or five participants or fewer. The more participants there are, the harder it will be to remain on track. It is also best to study with people who are not close friends so that you minimize distractions and off-topic conversations. When choosing members of your group, it is a good idea to discuss expectations for the group. If prospective members think that others will be helping them but they won't be contributing themselves, then they may not be right for your group. You will need members who will take on specific responsibilities that will benefit the whole group.

Once you have chosen your group participants, you should exchange contact information (phone and pager numbers and email addresses) and choose a leader.

Dennis MacDonald/PhotoEdit Inc.

One key to a successful study group is to limit the group to four or five participants.

The leader can change from meeting to meeting, but one person should be in charge of contacting everyone to announce the meeting time and place for the first session. The leader should also be responsible for keeping everyone on task if the group gets off topic and for assigning roles to each person, just as Juanita does for her group when she leads a study session.

When you meet with your group, be sure that each person contributes to the study session and "teaches" his or her assigned part. Periodically, the group should take breaks to keep people focused. To make studying comfortable, try to meet in a quiet location that allows food and drink; this way there will be fewer breaks and fewer people will be distracted by hunger or thirst. Also consider taking turns bringing snacks and beverages or chipping in for a meal. Better yet, go out for a meal *after* you study so that everyone has a goal to look forward to.

The difficulty of forming study groups in college is that many students lead full lives and have very little time to schedule extra activities. They also may not have consistent free time since they work different shifts each week or have different family responsibilities from day to day. To make your study group work, you may need to be creative about how you meet and how you organize your time. For example, you may want to join a chat room or use email to create a sample exam and "quiz" each other about the concepts on the exam.

General Tips for Study Groups

* Start with a small group of three to five people.
* Choose a leader for each meeting.
* Keep a master list of contact information.
* Schedule a time and place that is convenient, comfortable, and conducive to studying.
* Be creative about meeting. Try doing some of the work, such as creating sample test questions, through chat rooms or email.
* Assign each person a role in the group and part of the material to "teach" to the group.
* Do your "homework" before meeting by preparing to "teach" your material.
* Review your notes with each other.
* Quiz each other on the material before you leave your meeting.
* Be respectful of others' commitments.
* Take frequent breaks.
* Stay on task.
* Meet often for short periods of time rather than "marathon" sessions.

Types of Test Questions

Learning how to take tests will be just as important as learning the material. Knowing how to answer each type of possible test question will make taking an exam that much easier; at least, you will have less anxiety because you will know what to expect.

There are two categories of question types: objective and subjective. Objective questions can require lower-level thinking because they ask you to recall facts and concepts and usually appear in the form of multiple choice, true/false, fill-in-the-blank, and short answer. Subjective questions ask for your opinion about the material or ask you to apply the material in a new way. Essay and problem-solving (critical thinking) questions are labeled subjective because there are a variety of ways the questions can be answered correctly.

Sometimes, objective questions are easier to answer because they provide a correct answer within the choices. However, objective questions can demand significant brainpower, especially when you must recall an answer with very few clues, which is often the case with fill-in-the-blank questions. Because objective questions usually suggest only one correct answer, some students believe that there are no "wrong" answers for subjective questions, and that may be true, but there *are* better ways to answer them. In the following sections we discuss typical test questions and how to answer them.

Multiple Choice

Multiple-choice questions can test your recall of information or they can assess your ability to apply information or analyze situations. Despite their reputation for being easier, expect more difficult and time-consuming multiple-choice questions for college exams, and don't be alarmed if the answers are not obvious.

When answering multiple-choice questions, the first step is to read the question or statement carefully. Then, mark any special words in the question or statement such as "not," "always," and "only." Before looking at the choices, see if you can answer the question yourself. For example, consider the following multiple-choice question:

1. **What should you NOT do to alleviate anxiety when taking a test?** [Notice the word "NOT" and think in terms of what is not an acceptable answer.]

   A. **Arrive early for the exam.** [This is something you SHOULD do, so it is not the correct answer.]

   B. **Skip over the directions.** [This is something you should NOT do, so it may be the right answer. Keep reading the rest of the choices and lightly mark this one.]

   C. **Pay attention to the time limit.** [This is something you SHOULD do, so it is not the correct answer.]

   D. **Read all the questions before answering.** [Again, this is something you SHOULD do, so it is not the correct answer.]

After you have read through all the choices, the only correct answer is B. Consider another multiple-choice question:

2. **When answering an essay question on a test, be sure to**

   A. **Answer each part of the question thoroughly**. [This is something you should do. Keep reading the rest of the choices.]

B. **Organize your essay before writing it by sketching out a quick outline.** [This is something you should do. Keep reading the rest of the choices.]

C. **Read the directions carefully.** [Again, this is something you should do. Keep reading the rest of the choices to see if All of the Above is a choice since all the choices so far are good choices.]

D. **All of the above.** [This seems the best choice because all the other choices are correct.]

After you have read all the choices, D is the correct answer because it allows for A through C being correct.

When you are ready to answer the multiple-choice question, read each choice carefully and eliminate any answer that is obviously wrong. If you have to guess, eliminate any answer that is misspelled (usually a sign that the instructor has hurriedly added false answers) or any answer that is shorter than the others. Also, pay attention to choices labeled "All of the above" and "None of the above." If you can determine that at least two of the choices are correct, then "All of the above" is probably the correct answer. Likewise, if at least two of the choices are not correct, then "None of the above" is probably the correct answer.

Matching

A matching section on an exam presents you with two columns: a list of words or phrases that are to be matched with a list of descriptors. Professors who use matching sections usually require basic recall of information, but you will need to read the directions carefully. There may be more than one match for an item in the list or there may be extra descriptors.

To complete matching questions, first read through the entire list and choices to match before beginning. Then, determine if there could be multiple matches to a word in the list. Make sure that you have chosen the correct letter to match with each word in the list.

EXAMPLE OF MATCHING QUESTIONS

Match the following descriptions of interests and strengths with the appropriate multiple intelligences category. The categories may be used more than once; some may not be used at all.

____ 1. Enjoy outdoor activities

____ 2. Know how and why they act

____ 3. Good at design, architecture

____ 4. Choose careers in science, computer technology, engineering

____ 5. Use voice or instruments to express themselves

____ 6. Enjoy reading and writing

____ 7. Can read others' feelings well

____ 8. Fascinated with pictures

A. Verbal/linguistic

B. Logical/mathematical

C. Visual/spatial

D. Bodily/kinesthetic

E. Musical/rhythmic

F. Interpersonal

G. Intrapersonal

H. Naturalistic

True/False

True/false questions can be tough even though there are only two possible answers: true or false. Guessing or randomly answering true/false questions should be done as a last resort. It is better to read the statements carefully, noting key words that could point to the correct answer such as "frequently," "sometimes," and "a few." These words usually indicate a true statement. Words such as "never," "only," and "always" usually indicate a false statement.

If you have any difficulty answering true/false test questions, try not to confuse yourself with how the statement is worded. Go with your gut instinct. If are not entirely sure of what the statement is expressing, write down a justification of your answer on the test. Sometimes, professors will give partial credit if the wrong answer is clearly justified.

EXAMPLES OF TRUE/FALSE QUESTIONS

Determine if the statements are true or false. Circle the appropriate choice.

1. Howard Gardner's theory of multiple intelligences includes the category Nutritional/Health.
   - A. True
   - B. False
2. OK5R is a test-taking strategy.
   - A. True
   - B. False
3. Priorities are beliefs that can be shaped by experience and are not the same for everyone.
   - A. True
   - B. False
4. A mission statement is important because it declares your beliefs and your goals.
   - A. True
   - B. False
5. A priority is something that keeps you from achieving your goals.
   - A. True
   - B. False

Fill-in-the-Blank/Short Answer

Fill-in-the-blank and short answer questions require that you recall definitions of key terms or items in a series. To complete these types of questions, first read the sentence or question carefully. Often, points will be lost if you don't answer exactly or misspell the correct term.

EXAMPLES OF FILL-IN-THE-BLANK/SHORT ANSWER QUESTIONS

1. The T System for taking notes is also known as the _____.
2. Abbreviating words and phrases is called _____.
3. An instructor who is difficult to understand is an example of a listening _____.

4. _____ listening includes making the decision to concentrate on what is being said.

5. _____ is a method of note taking that involves numbering items and organizing them.

Problem Solving

Problem-solving, or critical thinking, questions are used by instructors so that students can demonstrate or apply the concepts or ideas they have learned. When you answer problem-solving questions, read the question carefully, marking multiple steps or parts to the directions. Next, determine what information you will need to solve the problem. Then, break the problem into parts and write down what process or operation you will need to perform. Work through the problem, and once you arrive at an answer, check the question again to make sure you have adequately answered it.

Here is an example of a problem-solving question, and an explanation for solving the problem follows:

> Beatrice has a scholarship that requires she maintain a 3.2 GPA while she is in college. During her first semester, she had 4 three-hour credit courses and made two A's and two B's. Now, she is taking one four-hour course and 4 three-hour courses. Can she make an A in her four-hour course and B's in her three-hour courses and keep her scholarship?

In order to answer this question correctly, you will need to know how to calculate GPA. If we break the steps down further, you will need to know the definition of grade points and quality points and how GPA is calculated when a student has taken classes for more than one semester. Then, you will need to know how to multiply, add, and divide. These sound like commonsense steps, but writing down every operation that you will need to perform will enable you to prepare to answer the question correctly and help you check the process by which you arrived at the answer.

EXAMPLE OF PROBLEM-SOLVING QUESTIONS

1. Lenise is taking a history class in which her grade is made up of four exams. So far she has made 65% and 74%. What are the lowest grades she can make to get a C in the course? Is it mathematically possible for her to earn a B?

2. In Carlos' biology class, the final grade is comprised of the following: homework (20%), midterm exam (30%), and final (50%). If Carlos makes 85% on his final, 71% on his midterm, and 68% for his homework grade, what is his final average?

3. Lester needs a 3.63 GPA to be inducted into the Phi Theta Kappa honor society. This semester, he has earned two C's, an A, and two B's in his courses (none of which have labs). Will he be inducted? Show your work below.

Essay

Instructors use essay questions to help them measure students' ability to analyze, synthesize, and evaluate the concepts they have learned; this type of question gauges more than students' recall of facts or terms. You can be assured that you will encounter more essay questions in college because they allow students to demonstrate a deeper understanding of the material.

One thing to remember about essay questions is that, although you won't have an enormous amount of time to complete an essay, your professor will still expect that you answer the essay question thoroughly and clearly. Always read the directions carefully. If the essay question has more than one part, be sure to mark each part and answer it in the body of the essay. If the directions specify a length, be sure to meet or exceed it. Before you begin writing, create a brief outline of what you will cover during the essay. Make a short list of transitions and details so that you can refer to the list if you get stuck during the exam.

Finally, because your professor will be reading and grading many essays, a clearly organized essay will stand out and make it easy for her to tell that you have discussed the key points. Just be sure to give yourself plenty of time to write the essay and use any remaining time you have to proofread and edit your work.

EXAMPLES OF ESSAY QUESTIONS

1. Do you think that colleges should strive, at whatever cost, to ensure that their campuses are diverse?

2. Do you think that colleges should prohibit personal and/or intimate relationships between professors and students? Explain your response and refer to the college's policy regarding student-professor relationships in your essay.

3. How have your relationships at home and at work changed since you have entered college?

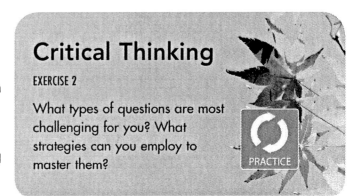

Critical Thinking

EXERCISE 2

What types of questions are most challenging for you? What strategies can you employ to master them?

PRACTICE

Types of Tests

Just as important as what types of questions you will encounter is what kind of test you can expect in different classes. For example, a math test will look quite different from a music test, and the strategies for studying for them and taking them will be different. Here we discuss a few different types of tests you may encounter in college. You may be able to apply the same tips to exams in other disciplines.

Math and Science Tests

For taking math and science tests, it is best to work through the problems you know first. Then, complete the problems that you do not know as well. If you complete your test early, consider reworking the test questions again on another sheet of paper and comparing your answers. If you discover two different answers for the same problem, figure out which answer contains the error. Always show your work and complete as many parts of a multiple-part problem as possible. You may receive partial credit for completing the process correctly even if you have not arrived at the right answer.

When answering questions on science tests that involve processes or major concepts, draw a picture to create a visual of the process and to help you answer questions about the steps. Regardless of what question types you will encounter, you will need to recall terms and definitions.

Fine Arts and Literature Tests

When taking exams in fine arts and literature classes, it is as important to explain the significance of the selected work, as it is to identify key passages, authors, terms, and eras. When taking exams in both disciplines, work through the easier questions first and save plenty of time for the writing portions. Think about the major themes and the historical importance of the works and look for those themes to be part of the questions on the test. While recall of facts about eras, dates, and creators of works will be part of the exam, there should be a significant emphasis on synthesizing the material.

Open-Book and Take-Home Tests

There will be occasions when you are given an open-book or take-home test. Although they sound as if they are the easiest kind of test to take, professors who hand out open-book tests make sure that you work hard to answer the questions correctly. In other words, these may be harder than in-class, closed-book exams. If you know ahead of time that you will be given an open-book exam, you will still need to study for it. Instead of spending too much time looking through your book and notes for the answers to the questions, you should be able to find the answers quickly. Chances are good that you will have many questions on an open-book exam to test how much you know about the subject. Likewise, take-home exams are often more difficult and time consuming than a regular test. At the least, your instructor will expect more from you if he allows you to take the test home to complete it. Because expectations are higher, you will need to give yourself plenty of time to formulate your answers and to check your work. Even though you will be unsupervised when writing the exam and probably expected to use a variety of resources for help, you will still need to maintain integrity. In other words, unless you receive permission from your instructor, do not accept or give help to other classmates.

Online Tests

Whether you take an online class or not, you may be required to take a quiz or test through an online learning system or through a website, such as a publisher's site that supports your textbook. Online tests are usually timed, which means you will need to keep an eye on how much time you have left after you answer each question. Instructors often place a time limit for online exams to discourage students from reviewing notes, going through the text, or surfing the Internet for answers. If your professor provides a practice test, consider taking it so that you can get a good feel for how much time you will have and what types of questions you will answer. Additional considerations include revisiting questions, if possible, to make sure you have not chosen the wrong answer for multiple-choice questions; ensuring that you have saved your answers before submitting your exam; and not sharing information about the exam to other students who have not taken it yet.

Comprehensive Exams

Comprehensive, or cumulative, exams are usually given during a week dedicated for "finals." Not all final tests are comprehensive—some professors choose to give their students shorter tests instead. However, most of the finals you will take in college will reflect the culmination of what you have learned all semester. Taking comprehensive exams at the end of the semester will seem like a daunting task if you have several classes, but there are some tips that will help you manage the task. First, it is important that you study for all your classes regularly. Reviewing notes daily will help you keep the information fresh. Second, make sure that you keep your notes and course materials organized so that you can easily find what you have covered throughout the semester. When you get closer to the date of your final exam, begin studying more intensely by reviewing the most current material and working backwards toward the material that was covered at the beginning of the semester.

Collaboration

Working within a group, brainstorm a list of tips that could help students study and take tests effectively. Divide your tips into categories that would help visual, aural, read/write, and kinesthetic learners.

EXERCISE 3

Test-Taking Strategies

Preparing for the Test

Before you begin to think about what is on a test and how you should study, you must make sure that you are taking care of yourself. Eating and sleeping are fundamental to doing well on tests. If you are not healthy, then you cannot perform at your highest level. Just as athletes prepare for performance days in advance by eating carbohydrates and resting, you should focus on getting regular sleep and eating well days before the exam. At the least, get a good night's rest the night before the test and avoid refined sugar (candy, cakes, and cookies) and caffeine.

Maintaining a good attitude as you prepare for the exam is another effective strategy. Monitor and eliminate any negative self-talk about your ability to do well on exams. Instead, visualize yourself taking the test successfully and earning a good grade.

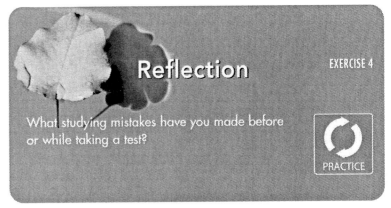

Reflection

EXERCISE 4

What studying mistakes have you made before or while taking a test?

PRACTICE

Taking the Test

Once you have prepared for the test, both physically and mentally, you should be ready to take it. Before you leave for class, be sure that you have the appropriate supplies: Will you need a watch, paper, pen, pencil, a calculator, or a dictionary and thesaurus? Are there any approved test-taking aids that you need to bring as well? Will you be able to use your textbook or a cheat sheet with formulas on it? Once you arrive in class, take a seat away from distractions and where you feel comfortable to spread out and get to work. If you are not wearing a watch, sit somewhere you will be able to see a clock. Cell phone access, which many students use to keep track of time, may be restricted during tests, so be sure to keep track of time some other way. When taking tests that use a Scantron or bubble form in which you have to pencil in your answers by filling in circles, be sure to bring at least two sharpened pencils.

When you first get the test, read through all the questions, noting which ones will take longer to answer than the others. Taking that time to read all the questions is actually a time saver, because you will know what to expect and how to pace yourself. Turn the paper over and check out the back. Your instructor may have made two-sided copies of the test, which means you will have questions on the back and front of the paper.

As you read through the test, make note of the types of questions and use the tips in this chapter to answer them. Read the directions for each section carefully and mark any special instructions. For example, in a matching section, there may be more than one match for an item in one of the columns; in an essay writing section, there may be a choice of topics. Also, be aware of how many points each section is worth. If one section is worth half the points for the entire exam, you will need to spend a majority of your time working that part.

Pacing yourself during the exam is very important. Before you begin the test, you should determine how much time you need to spend on each section based on the types of questions, your comfort level with the questions, and the amount of points it is worth. As a general rule, you should spend less than a minute per multiple choice and true/false questions and 15 minutes or more to answer essay questions. For the other types of questions, you will need to spend somewhere in between 1 and 5 minutes. If you get off track and spend too much time on one section, don't panic. You will just need to work quickly and carefully on the rest of the exam.

Working the easiest questions first, mark questions that you don't know the answer to or that you find confusing. Don't come back to them until you have completed all the questions that you can easily answer. If you are unsure of an answer, mark that question as well and plan to review it before turning in your exam. If the question or problem has multiple parts, work through as many of the parts that you can. Do not leave questions unanswered. Partial answers may receive partial credit unless you have been instructed otherwise.

Finally, leave yourself 5–10 minutes to check your work. If you finish an exam early, always go back through the questions and go over your answers by ensuring that all questions are answered and that all parts are completed. If you have written an essay, read through your response and check for grammatical, spelling, and punctuation errors. Initial each page and number the pages of your essay, if appropriate. Turn in your exam and any paper on which you worked problems or drafted an essay.

Maintaining Integrity During the Test

You may have recently read about the new lengths that students go to in order to cheat on exams or to plagiarize. Advances in technology have made cheating easier and have made it seem more widespread. Although there is no clear evidence that more students are cheating now than they were 30 years ago, there does seem to be more confusion about what constitutes cheating. For example, some professors require group presentations and collaboration on projects; however, very few offer guidelines on who should do what and how to document the part that each student does. In addition, collaboration on homework assignments, which was encouraged in high school, may now be prohibited in college. When in doubt about how you should complete homework or group projects, ask your instructor for specific guidelines.

The integrity rules are a little clearer when taking a test. Unless otherwise stated, do not use notes, books, or classmates as references for the exam. Most instructors will ask you to clear your desk of any material except paper and a pen or will ask you to move away from the nearest person. All of these actions are to ensure that there are no questions about the originality of the work. Other instructors are more trusting of students and may leave the classroom or give the class a take-home test. An instructor who allows such freedom is sending you a message about integrity: He trusts that his students will act maturely, responsibly, and honestly. Violating that trust can have grave consequences because not only does the cheating student create problems for herself, but she has also damaged the relationship of trust for the entire class.

To ensure that you act with integrity when taking an exam, whether supervised or not, do your own work and keep your work surface clear of books, papers, folders, cell phones, pagers, and even drink bottles. If possible, distance yourself from other students so that they are less likely to cheat off you. If you are ever in doubt, however, about your actions or the requirements for an exam, be sure to ask your professor.

Beating Test Anxiety

All of the information in this chapter is difficult to put into practice if you have overwhelming anxiety about taking tests. It is not unusual to experience nervousness, anxiety, and fear before or during a test, but extreme anxiety accompanied by excessive sweating, nausea, and crying is not normal. If you are experiencing conditions that make taking and completing tests impossible, you should see a college counselor or other professional. However, if you occasionally experience very mild conditions, there are some techniques that can help minimize your anxiety and fear. Remember that some degree of nervousness is normal and can actually give you an adrenaline boost.

In order to cope with mild anxiety, there are a variety of activities you can do to relieve tension. Basic relaxation techniques such as deep breathing and visualizations can take the edge off the tension of taking a test. Taking the time to breathe deeply whenever you feel overwhelmed will help you stay in control. Also, visualizing yourself relaxing or succeeding at a test can help you get beyond self-defeating doubt and stress.

INTEGRITY MATTERS

According to Dr. Donald McCabe at the Center for Academic Integrity, 75% of college students admit to some cheating. Almost 25% have admitted to serious cheating, and nearly 50% admitted to cheating in one or more instances.

Source: "CAI Research." Retrieved August 2, 2005, from www.academicintegrity.org/cai_research.asp.

PLUS

(Personality + Learning Style = Understanding Situations)

Let's revisit the study group's discussion. Juanita, the youngest, learns best by writing and has severe test anxiety, while Michael is visual and needs more direction in what to study. Evan, a kinesthetic learner, has gotten by with little studying in the past, and Laura learns best when she hears information, but she has been distracted with other obligations. What study strategies and test-taking tips can each use?

Now, considering your own learning style, personality type, and special circumstances, what would you do if you were studying with fellow students whose own learning styles and levels of preparation differ from your own?

PROFILE

MY STORY
Learning Plan

Directions: Using what you have learned in this chapter and what you know about your learning preferences, choose a task or assignment that needs to be completed soon and create a learning plan that will help you accomplish this task. Then, write your *My Story* Summary, a one-sentence synopsis that crystallizes your newly created plan.

LEARNING TASK	
Time of Day	
Intake Preference	
Social Preference	
Task Management Preference	

MY STORY SUMMARY:

Path of Discovery

How do you study best for tests? How did you develop these study habits? What do you want to change, if anything, about how you prepare for an exam?

HOMEWORK

From College to University

How Studying and Testing May Differ after Transfer

As you take upper-level classes, you may find that tests and papers seem to get fewer and farther between, but their importance to the overall course is greater. Your reading load will increase and the subject matter will get more technical. You may also find yourself reading a variety of material: textbooks, journal articles, lab manuals, dissertations, novels, surveys, charts, graphs, and statistics.

Your critical thinking skills will be essential to making it through these courses. Your professors will also expect that you have strong study skills and solid test-taking strategies because they will provide few clues as to what you will be tested on and how you will be tested. This is not to say that university professors are cold and uncaring about your learning; instead, because they are concerned with pushing your abilities in terms of thinking and learning, they may have little time for helping you improve your study skills.

If you have a solid foundation of skills and strategies, then you will be successful. You will just need to monitor your progress and make adjustments as necessary. For instance, while you may not have studied with a group before, at the university, you may find that study groups are essential for covering the massive amounts of material. Your goal should be finding what works best for you and what continues to help you succeed.

From College to Career

Preparation Counts

Just as you will prepare for exams and presentations in college, you will use the same skills on the job. Time management, attention to detail, and careful preparation will be necessary to be successful in your career. Depending on your career choice, you may have to pass proficiency tests or certification exams at least once or even once a year. Failing an exam in college may not mean the end of your academic career, but failing a licensing exam or a certification test could very well be the end of your job. Thus, the stakes—and the stress—will be much higher on the job.

Although the pressure to pass will be greater, chances are good that since you have been to college and passed many tests, your test-taking skills will get you through exams on the job. In addition to reviewing the test-taking strategies that are outlined in this chapter, you should also take advantage of any test preparation seminars that your employer offers. Also, now is the time to demonstrate your ability to study with others. There is no better study group than your coworkers because they all have the same investment as you: They want to pass the exam in order to keep their jobs or advance to a higher position.

Chapter Review Questions

1. What kinds of study strategies will benefit visual, aural, read/write, and kinesthetic learners?

2. What kinds of questions can you expect to be asked on science tests? On literature tests?

3. Compare studying in a group with studying on your own. What are the benefits of both? What are the drawbacks?

4. In what ways can a student beat test anxiety?

Case Scenarios

1. Sylvia's accounting professor has announced to his class that he allows students to study from old tests. In fact, he keeps a folder of previous exams in the library for students to access. One of Sylvia's classmates asks her if she wants to study for the test, and she agrees. When they meet, her classmate pulls out a copy of a test with the current semester's date on it. Sylvia questions her classmate, who says that the professor gave her a rough draft of a test that he decided not to use. When Sylvia gets to class, she recognizes every question because it is the same test that her classmate had. What should Sylvia do?

2. Ryan does not think he knows how to study well. He glided through high school without cracking open a book. Now, he is in college and taking five classes: Intermediate Algebra, Reading Improvement, Introduction to Sociology, Speech Communication, and Concepts of Health and Wellness. He is struggling through his health and math classes. What can you tell him about studying for those subjects that will help him get back on track?

3. Betty gets sweaty palms and wants to throw up each time she takes a test. She has failed classes before because she couldn't calm herself down enough to take a major test. This semester, though, Betty wants to do better because she cannot keep dropping or failing her classes. What advice can you give Betty that will help ease her fears? What can she do and what kind of help can she get so that she can be successful?

Research It Further

1. Investigate methods of cheating that have occurred with "high-stakes" testing such as licensure and college-entrance exams. Write a report about these methods and the effects that they have had on how organizations test.

2. What are the most popular ways that students study at your college? Create a questionnaire that asks students how, when, and where they study. Once you tally the results, determine whether the students at your college need a one-page reminder of how to study effectively. If you think they do, create one based on the shortcomings of their methods of studying.

3. Using the material in this chapter, create two or three games that can help students remember and understand the material.

References

Klauser, H. A. (2001). *Write it down, make it happen: Knowing what you want and getting it!* New York: Simon & Schuster.

Planning for Next Semester

5

From Chapter 11 of *The Community College Experience Plus*, Second Edition, Amy Baldwin.
Copyright © 2010 by Pearson Education, Inc. Published by Pearson Prentice Hall. All rights reserved.

Planning for Next Semester

Juanita and Laura's Story

"Hey, Laura, who are you taking for world history?" asks Juanita as she squints in the bright sun outside the library. Laura pulls out a sheet of paper with her schedule for next semester. Her brightly painted nails catch the sunlight and look like twinkling stars.

"I have Dr. Franks," she says. "I interviewed him and Professor Martinsen last week to see which one would be a good fit for me." Laura takes a moment to take off her jacket and stuffs it in her backpack while Juanita checks her phone to see if her mother has called her, a daily ritual that she has been able to lessen as she has taken classes on the college campus. When Juanita was in high school, she talked to her mother four or five times a day.

"Really? I just checked out that website where you can write about your instructors. I think I want Mr. Bernstein's class. He makes you do a group project rather than take an exam—at least that is what they say about him," Juanita says.

"It's hard to get a good picture just from an Internet site, don't you think? I think you should go talk to him first. How do you know what he is like as a person?" asks Laura, frowning at her friend. Because of Laura's dyslexia, she spends much more time rewriting her notes and working on assignments than her fellow students. Getting professors that she feels comfortable with is important to her. She knows she is not as technologically savvy as the younger students, but sometimes she thinks finding things out the "old-fashioned way" is best.

"Maybe I need to find someone who can also help me with my degree plan. I am still unsure about what I want to major in. I know I am only 18, but I need to get this decided soon," Juanita says. Her phone vibrates. She has a new message, but it is from her cousin, not her mother.

"Are you still worried that your parents are going to be upset if you choose something other than engineering or medicine?" Laura asks. She feels lucky that even at her age, her mother encourages her to do what she wants.

"Probably, but now that I am 18, I guess I don't have to worry about my mom calling my advisor to tell him what I should major in," Juanita says, smiling at Laura and shading her eyes from the sun.

"I tell you what. Pick up your things and come with me. I need to go to counseling anyway. I am worried about my scholarship for next semester and I need to know, if I bomb our final in biology, what I should do," says Laura.

Juanita gathers her books and stuffs them in her backpack. She follows Laura to the campus center, hoping to get some answers to her questions about how she should plan not only her next semester, but also her life. As they walk across campus, Juanita's phone rings again, and she sees that it is her mother this time.

In This Chapter

The purpose of this chapter is to help you navigate the last few weeks of classes and to help you plan your semesters to come. As both Laura and Juanita remind us, these last weeks will be filled with decisions to make about finances and course work, but once you have successfully completed a certificate or degree program you will be able to say, "I did it!" This chapter provides information that will enable you to:

* Identify how to prepare for the end of the semester and what to expect.

* Recognize the steps for planning for next semester.

* Determine the steps to complete your education at this college or another.

* Identify methods for paying for college.

Endings and Beginnings

By the time you start reading this chapter, you may have completed most of your first semester and perhaps even have been thinking about next semester and beyond. The end of the semester is a good time to start assessing how you have done and where you want to go. Before you can begin planning for next semester, there will be some loose ends to tie up for your current semester. You should now know what to expect at the beginning of next semester, and with that additional information, you should be able to make better choices and prepare yourself for what lies ahead.

Course Evaluations

Course evaluations (sometimes called "student" evaluations because students evaluate the course and the instructor) by students are an integral part of taking a college class. Each semester you may be asked to complete an evaluation form for your instructor. The evaluations are anonymous and are not given to the instructor until grades have been posted; thus, you should feel comfortable being open and honest about the course when answering the form's questions.

The purpose of course evaluations is to provide the instructor as well as the administration with a description of how students feel about the instruction they received in the course. Some colleges look very closely at course evaluations and determine raises and promotions based in part on the scores that instructors receive. Other colleges merely use it as a discussion tool to improve the instructors' teaching. No matter how your college uses the information, you should try to be honest about your instructors' abilities. Providing constructive criticism, rather than general comments, is most helpful to the instructor.

Phrases such as "Professor Banks is not a good instructor" or "Dr. Wright is perfect" do not provide specific information that will help your instructor improve or help him or her to continue doing what you think works very well. Instead, you may want to offer comments such as "The instructor graded fairly and handed back exams in a timely manner" or "The professor rarely explained the assignments." These statements allow your instructors to pinpoint exactly what worked for you and what didn't.

Most student evaluation forms contain questions that you answer by checking a box or filling in a bubble as well as questions that you answer by writing a narrative response. Here are examples of two types of questions that you may see on a course evaluation form:

1. My instructor uses class time effectively.

   A. Strongly Agree B. Agree C. Strongly Disagree

2. My instructor grades fairly.

   A. Strongly Agree   B. Agree   C. Strongly Disagree

3. What can your instructor do to improve the course? _____

4. What does your instructor do well? _____

When answering questions such as these, take time to reflect on the instructor's performance during the semester. Create a list of activities that you did in class during the semester and think about them. Then, consider the overall performance of your instructor. Did he come to class on time? Was she easy to contact when you needed her? Did he act professionally? Did she seem to have a good knowledge of the subject matter? Remember that the objective of student evaluations is to provide feedback that will help instructors improve, so the more information you provide, the better.

Preparing for Final Examinations

Another traditional "ending" to the semester is final exams. Surviving "finals week" is often considered a well-earned badge of a college student. The reason that finals are so stressful for some college students is that they often carry more weight than any other tests during the semester, they contain questions about material from the entire semester, and they are all scheduled around the same time.

There are steps you can follow to get ready for finals quickly in these final weeks of the semester. First, be sure to note the day, place, and time of each final and write it down on your calendar. Double-check this information a week before the exam. Be aware that where and when you take your finals may differ from where and when you took your classes during the semester.

A few weeks before the final, ask questions about the exam. What will you be allowed to use? What do you need to bring? What should you study? Is photo identification required? Get plenty of rest during the days that lead up to the exam. When you take the exam, use your time wisely. Final exams usually take longer to complete than regular tests, so be sure you use the entire time that you are allotted (one to three hours). Be prepared by bringing ample writing supplies and any approved items such as a calculator or dictionary.

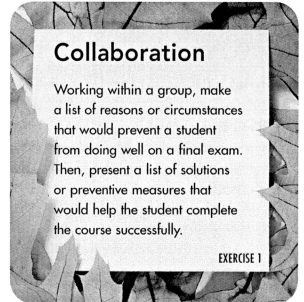

Collaboration

Working within a group, make a list of reasons or circumstances that would prevent a student from doing well on a final exam. Then, present a list of solutions or preventive measures that would help the student complete the course successfully.

EXERCISE 1

Mapping a Plan for Your Educational Future

A Difference of Degrees

You probably discovered when you enrolled that community colleges offer a variety of certificate and degree options, but you may not be entirely clear about the differences between those programs. Certificate programs usually last a semester or two semesters (sometimes referred to as "one year" programs) and require about 15 to 30 credit hours. Students enroll in certificate programs either to gain skills to enter the workforce or to complete training requirements for a job. Most certificate programs are not transferable, which means they do not necessarily meet the requirements of an associate's or bachelor's degree. Instead, they usually serve a specific purpose of providing graduates with a set of skills that they can readily use on the job. If you plan to use a certificate program as a stepping-stone for an associate's or bachelor's degree, be sure that you check with the department or college (if it is not the same as the one in which you are currently enrolled) where you will complete your final degree plan. For example, if you want to complete a bachelor's degree in nursing, but you are thinking about completing a nursing certificate first, talk to an advisor in the bachelor's program to determine what, if any, courses they can take from your certificate program. Although you may choose, for personal or professional reasons, to earn a certificate first and then take additional classes to complete another degree, knowing what will be accepted and what will not can help you make the best educational decisions now.

In addition to certificate programs, community colleges offer associate of arts (A.A.), associate of science (A.S.), and associate of applied science (A.A.S.) degrees (see Table 1). Unlike certificate programs, an associate's degree usually requires that a student take twice as many credit hours, at least 60. Associate of arts and associate of science degrees more closely mirror the first two years of a bachelor's degree and are often transferable to a four-year university with little problem. Nonetheless, as with any degree program, always check with the institution from which you will graduate last to make sure that the classes you take for your associate's degree fulfill the requirements of the bachelor's program. Other associate degrees include associate of fine arts (A.F.A.) and associate of arts in teaching (A.A.T.).

The associate of applied science degree is different because it is a 60-hour (at least) program that is intended for students who plan on entering the workforce after graduation; it is not usually intended for students who want to transfer to complete a bachelor's degree, although some four-year universities are beginning to accept courses that are completed in this degree program. An associate of applied science in accounting degree, for example, is meant for students who want an entry-level job in bookkeeping. To earn a bachelor's degree in accounting, however, a student would earn an associate of arts degree that will fit into the bachelor of science in accounting degree at a university.

Choosing the right certificate or degree program will take some thought and discussion with college advisors, people in the career you want or already have, and your instructors. Ultimately, your career and life goals will determine which program to choose. Remember that no matter which certificate or degree you complete, you

TABLE 1   Program Types

Program Type	Length/Requirements	Purpose
Certificate	One semester or two; 15–30 credit hours	To obtain skills necessary for a job-related or personal goal or for direct entry into the workforce; not intended to fit into a higher degree
Associate of Applied Science	Four semesters; about 60 credit hours	To obtain knowledge and skills for direct entry into the workforce; usually not intended to fit into a higher degree
Associate of Arts/Sciences	Four semesters; about 60 credit hours	To obtain knowledge and skills for transfer to a higher degree program or for direct entry into the workforce

can always return to college at any time to continue your education. With the fluctuations in job requirements, changes in industry, and longer life spans, you may find yourself back in college again at some point in your life to learn a new skill, change your life's direction, or dabble in a hobby.

Exhibit 1 shows an example of a degree program that Laura may consider.

This degree plan is relatively simple to follow. However, Laura may be a little confused if she has to take prerequisites before she can take some of the courses. For example, when Laura entered college, her ACT test scores placed her below college entrance requirements; thus, she had to complete her developmental courses before she could take some of the college-level courses that are part of her degree program.

So, how does Laura plan for next semester? In her first semester, if Laura completes Introduction to College (a three-hour credit course), Developmental Reading

EXHIBIT 1   Degree Plan

EARLY CHILDHOOD DEVELOPMENT [THE DEPARTMENT]

Associate of Applied Science [*type of degree—usually completed in four semesters*]

Option: Early Childhood Education [*the emphasis within the degree*]

This option is for early childhood caregivers and paraprofessionals who wish to improve their skills and credentials. Early childhood curriculum is the focus. This option is also appropriate for supervisors, for curriculum coordinators, and for CDA renewal. [*description of how this degree will benefit you*]

[*Suggested schedule for each semester. It is usually not mandatory that you take the courses in the order that they suggest, unless one is a prerequisite for another.*]

FIRST SEMESTER		CREDIT HOURS
ECD 1003	Foundations of Early Childhood Education	3
ECD 1103	Child Development	3
ECD 1203	Healthy, Safe Learning Environment	3
ECD 1303	Practicum I	3
ENGL 1311	English Composition I	3
Total Credit Hours		15

SECOND SEMESTER		
ECD 2003	Child Behavior	3
ECD 2103	Preschool Curriculum, or	

(continued)

ECD 2403	Infant/Toddler Curriculum	3
ECD 2503	Nutrition for the Young Child	3
ECD 2303	Practicum II	3
MATH 1301	College Business Mathematics	3
Total Credit Hours		15

THIRD SEMESTER

ECD 2703	Language Arts	3
ECD 2803	Special Needs	3
ENGL 1312	English Composition II	3
PSYC 2300	Psychology and the Human Experience	3
HLSC 1304	Concepts of Lifetime Health and Wellness, or	
MUSC 2300	Introduction to Music, or	
ARTS 2300	Introduction to Visual Arts	3
Total Credit Hours		15

FOURTH SEMESTER

ECD 2903	Trends in Curriculum	3
BUS 1303	Introduction to Computers or higher-level computer course	3
SOCI 2300	Introduction to Sociology	3
SPCH 1300	Speech Communication	3
ANTH 2310	Cultural Anthropology, or	
PSYC 2300	Developmental Psychology	3
Total Credit Hours		15
Total Hours for A.A.S.		60

(receives no college-level credit), Developmental Writing (receives no college-level credit), Introduction to Sociology (a three-hour credit course), and Psychology and the Human Experience (a three-hour credit course), then she has already met two of the requirements for an associate of applied science degree in early childhood education. She would check those courses off her degree plan and start working toward the remaining courses as long as she has met the developmental requirements for them.

An example of Laura's schedule for next semester may look like the following:

ENGL 1311 English Composition I	3 hours
ECD 1103 Child Development	3 hours
ECD 1003 Foundations of Early Childhood Education	3 hours
PSYC 2300 Psychology and the Human Experience	3 hours
ECD 1203 Healthy, Safe Learning Environment	3 hours
	15 hours

If Laura takes 15 hours her second semester and 15 hours each semester after that, she still will need to take an extra semester, because in her first semester she earned only 6 hours toward her degree. Even though the early childhood associate's degree plan maps out four semesters, for some students it may take longer to complete because they need to take fewer hours per semester or they have to complete developmental classes. These are things you will need to consider as you map out your degree program.

Choosing Classes and Professors for Next Semester

Even if you have not completed your classes this semester, you can start planning for next semester. By now, you should be familiar with the college catalog and can identify the courses that you may want to take.

Just as important as what classes you take next semester is with whom you take those classes. By now, you should realize that choosing the right instructor could make the difference in how much you enjoy and learn in a class. If you have the option of choosing an instructor, then you should start talking with other students about them. Ask specific questions and ask a variety of people. Remember that each student has his or her own view of what makes a good instructor, a view that might not match your own. Questions you should ask need to move beyond the vague "Is she a good teacher?" Instead, you should ask about her teaching style, the types of assignments she gives, and how available she is during office hours. Be wary of Internet sites that rate professors. They are not reliable because anyone can post just about anything they want without regard to accuracy, or sometimes decency. There is no mechanism to keep the same people from posting multiple positive or negative comments, which can present only part of the picture.

An even better way to determine which instructors are the best for you is to talk with them before you enroll in their classes. Make an appointment with a potential instructor and ask pertinent questions: How much reading is involved? How do you teach the course? Do you require a research paper? What do you expect students to know when they complete the course? The benefits of interviewing your instructor before you sign up for the class are that you get to determine whether the instructor is a good fit with your learning style and you get to make a good impression by demonstrating your maturity and interest in your education.

Building Your Schedule

What worked this semester and what didn't? Why? What will change for you next semester? Did you have enough time in between classes? Did you waste time that could have been spent more productively? You will need to answer all of these questions before you set your schedule for next semester.

When planning your next semester (and beyond), consider four factors: how many hours you need to take, how many hours you need to work, what other obligations (planned trips for work or with family, for example) you have, and how much stress these three factors will cause.

- *Number of credit hours.* To determine how many credit hours you need to take, be sure to review your financial aid, scholarship, and degree plan information. If you are receiving financial aid, you may be required to take a full load, which often means at least 12 hours. As you can see in the previous example, Laura needed to take 15 hours each semester in order to finish her degree in four semesters. However, because she had to take developmental classes her first semester, she only met 6 hours of the required courses for her associate's degree.

- *Number of work hours.* If you will not be working next semester, you can skip this section. However, even if you are only working a few hours a week, you will need to schedule your work hours so that they do not overlap with the times you are in class. You also need to allow plenty of time to get to and from work and school. Be realistic when calculating this time and plan for delays. An accurately planned schedule will help keep your stress levels at a minimum.

- *Amount of learning support and learning opportunities.* If you know or anticipate a need for learning assistance or tutoring, be sure to build that time into your schedule. You may also need to see each of your professors on a regular basis, some more than others, which should also be a consideration when creating a schedule. If you leave little time for meeting with your instructors, it will be difficult to get the help and advice you need. Good time management and a flexible schedule will allow plenty of time for visits to the computer lab to get help with sending an attachment to an email, to the library for assistance in using the databases, and to the tutoring lab at the hours and locations that are most convenient to you.

Laima Druskis/PH College

Letting others know what you plan to take next semester and how that will affect them will create less stress for you in the long run.

- *Other obligations.* Working, going to school, taking care of a family, and participating in social and community activities all require your time and energy. To balance all your activities, you will need to keep an eye on upcoming events and make sure you plan accordingly. For example, if you are thinking about registering for the fall semester and you know that you must take a weeklong trip for work in October, you should contact potential instructors to see what their policies are for missing class. Likewise, if you like to participate in your child's school activities, you will need to consider how much time you can give if you are also studying for classes.

You may find that you need to cut back on social and volunteer commitments or at least postpone them until after the semester.

- *Stress levels.* Your work schedule, course load, and other responsibilities can lead to high levels of stress. For example, if you have to take 15 hours of courses to maintain your financial aid and you have to work 40 hours to pay your bills, but you feel overwhelmed and anxious about balancing it all, then you are not likely to handle both well. If you find yourself in this situation, you will need to reconsider your plans before you get in over your head. Getting locked into a rigid schedule that doesn't allow you to drop a course that is too difficult or to decrease your hours at work will lead to frustration and high levels of negative stress.

On the other hand, you may thrive on such a schedule because you work better when you have to manage your time carefully. You may be the type of person who cannot study well if you have unlimited amounts of time to do it. If this is the case, you may feel excited about having so much activity in your schedule. Still, you could encounter a problem in which having flexibility (being able to drop a class or reducing your work hours) will help you cope. If you don't have this flexibility, then you need to pay extra attention to staying on top of your work. For example, if you find on the first day of the semester that one of your classes will be much more demanding than you had anticipated, you will need to be more careful about keeping up with assignments and managing your stress effectively. Planning ahead and managing your time will help you cope with a stressful schedule.

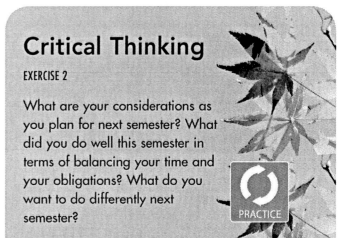

Critical Thinking

EXERCISE 2

What are your considerations as you plan for next semester? What did you do well this semester in terms of balancing your time and your obligations? What do you want to do differently next semester?

PRACTICE

Troubleshooting Your Schedule

What should you do if you cannot work your schedule out despite your efforts to make it all fit together? There may be a semester in which a course you need is not offered or the class is filled before you can register. Should you throw up your hands and quit when faced with these problems? Of course not. Instead, you should take advantage of the relationships you have cultivated at college. Now is the time to talk with fellow students, instructors, and advisors. They may be able to offer solutions that you have not considered. If, however, there is an academic need for you to get into a class or rearrange your schedule, you should point that out. Some college officials are willing to bend the rules if you need one more class to complete your degree and transfer on time.

Deadlines and Dates

Once you decide on your schedule and the classes you want to take, you should take advantage of early registration periods and due dates. If there is even a small chance you will return next semester, consider registering for courses just in case. Depending on your college's policies, you should be able to drop courses by a certain date without penalty, and it will be easier to drop classes than build a schedule from classes that are still open. In addition to being aware of registration periods, take note of payment due dates. Some colleges require that you pay soon after you register, even if that means paying for tuition and fees a few months in advance. If you do not pay on time, your classes may be dropped, and you will have to start all over right before the new semester, which could mean that you don't get the classes for which you originally registered.

Mapping a Plan for Your Financial Future

Paying for College

When thinking about your financial future, most likely paying for college will be at the top of your list. Even if you have a solid plan for paying tuition, fees, and books, it will be worth your time to investigate other methods in case your current one falls through. Despite what many think about the costs of college, community college tuition is a real bargain and perhaps one of the reasons that you enrolled. Regardless of where you choose to go to school, it is likely that you will need to decide how you will pay for the costs you incur.

Scholarships

Winning a scholarship is by far the most rewarding way (financially and psychologically) to pay for college because it is literally free money—you don't have to pay it back. There are thousands of scholarships out there for needy and accomplished students. All you have to do is find them. To find the ones that match your profile, you will need to get the word out that you are looking. Talking with friends, family, employers, and college officials is a great way to start the process. They may know of obscure scholarships that will fit your needs perfectly.

Another way to get information about scholarships is to talk with the financial aid officers and counselors at your college. They have access to and knowledge of scholarships that fit the college's student profiles such as single-parent and transfer scholarships that will pay your tuition and fees at a four-year university. Other effective methods for finding scholarships are to investigate sources at your library and search the Internet. Searching print and Web-based databases will provide you with more than enough information; the only problem will be narrowing your focus.

Whatever information about scholarships you find—whether it's in books, in counselors' offices, or on the Internet—don't pay for it. Some services claim to match your qualifications with scholarship qualifications but charge a fee to do so. You can get free help from high school and college counselors as well as libraries and Internet searches. No reputable scholarship service will require that you pay a fee to apply, and very few scholarship services will require payment. The website FinAid! (www.finaid.org) provides information about different types of financial aid for college students as well as tips for avoiding scholarship services scams. According to this site, any service that guarantees to match you with a scholarship or that offers you an award that you did not apply for is likely to be a scam. Many colleges recommend www.fastweb.com as a great starting point for finding scholarships that match your accomplishments.

Grants

By definition, grants are financial assistance that does not need to be paid back. A common federal grant is the Pell grant, which can be awarded for full-time or part-time enrollment. To determine your eligibility, talk with your financial aid counselor or visit any of the various websites that provide government information about financial aid. When you research Pell grants, you will find that there is a limit to the amount of the award ($4,310 in 2007–2008) and that your college will receive the money and then disburse it to you once classes start. Because of recent federal requirements about grants and student loans, colleges may wait several weeks before paying students. If you are expecting to receive your grant the first day or week of classes, you should make alternative arrangements to pay bills (including your bookstore bill).

Another type of grant that a student can receive is the Federal Supplemental Educational Opportunity Grant (FSEOG), which is available to those who demonstrate an exceptional need. According to the U.S. Department of Education (2008), the difference between a Pell grant and an FSEOG is that "each participating school will receive enough money to pay the federal Pell grants of its eligible students. There's no guarantee every eligible student will be able to receive an FSEOG." The procedure for receiving an FSEOG is similar to that for receiving a Pell grant; your eligibility will determine the amount that you receive, and your college will disburse the money to you after the semester begins.

In addition to payment schedules, you will need to maintain good academic standing at your college to remain eligible to receive grant money. If you apply for a grant, be sure to make note of the minimum GPA that you must have in order to ensure your eligibility to receive future grant money. One last tip for continuing to receive grant funding: Make sure that you adhere to the college's attendance policy. You may be penalized (and lose your grant funding or have to pay it back) for missing too many classes or for dropping a class. As always, check with your financial aid officer to make sure that you clearly understand the expectations for receiving grants.

Student Loans

In the event that you are not eligible for grants, you should investigate student loans. The idea of taking out a loan to attend college makes many students shudder with fear because they don't want the added pressure that they must pay back what they borrow. If you can avoid a student loan, then by all means do so. However, receiving a student loan sometimes makes more financial sense in the long run.

Federal student loans typically charge low interest and can be paid back over 10 years. For families that would otherwise have to deplete their savings or borrow against retirement or their mortgages to pay for college, a low-interest student loan is a good option. Most loan programs allow you to defer payment (but you may accumulate interest) until after you graduate, or you can sometimes defer payment if you remain unemployed after you graduate.

One type of federal loan is the Stafford loan, which comes in subsidized and unsubsidized versions. A subsidized loan is one in which the government pays the interest for you while you are in college. Once you graduate and start making payments on your loan, you will accrue interest as well. The government does not make interest payments for an unsubsidized loan; however, you may, instead, pay the interest while you are in college (usually a small amount), or you can wait until after you graduate to make any payments, but your interest will be capitalized. In other words, the interest will be added to the principal amount of the loan, which makes your monthly payments higher.

A federal Perkins loan is a loan between you and your college. The Perkins loan allows you to borrow $4,000 per year up to $20,000 for 5 years, and you don't have to repay it until 9 months after you graduate or drop below at least part-time status.

One benefit of a Perkins loan is that you may be able to cancel up to 100 percent of the debt if you meet certain criteria. For example, upon graduation, if you choose to teach in a "teacher shortage" area or if you serve as a full-time nurse, you may be eligible for cancellation of your loan.

PLUS, which stands for Parent Loan for Undergraduate Students, is another method of receiving money to help pay for college. If you are fortunate enough to have parents willing to take out a loan to help you pay for college, a PLUS is a possible option. To qualify, you must be a dependent student, which means your parents support you financially. A PLUS can be provided by the government or by private lenders. Parents who take out a PLUS are usually trying to make up the difference between the cost of tuition and the financial aid package that their children receive. Nonetheless, it is the parents who are ultimately responsible for repaying the loan, which can be as early as 60 days after they receive it.

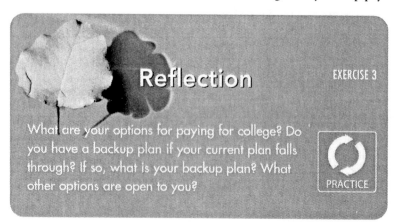

Reflection

EXERCISE 3

What are your options for paying for college? Do you have a backup plan if your current plan falls through? If so, what is your backup plan? What other options are open to you?

PRACTICE

Military and Veterans Financial Aid

Being a member of the military can be especially helpful when you are paying for college. There are numerous benefits for active members and veterans as well as their dependents. To find out about military benefits, talk with a financial aid officer. If you have served in the military, you may want to contact a local service branch for more information as well.

Work-Study

Work-study is a program that allows students to earn money while they work on campus. The reason it is called "work-study" is that the job may allow for you to study when you work, but most work-study positions are similar to office assistants and will

INTEGRITY MATTERS

Student loans, because they charge low interest and have a long-term payment plan, are often a good way to pay for college if you do not have the financial means to do so otherwise. However, there are serious consequences if you do not pay them back when you are required to do so. Defaulting on student loans can make you ineligible for future federal aid and can have negative consequences on your credit rating. Before you sign to receive a student loan, be sure that you have a plan to pay it back after you graduate. And if you find yourself unable to make a payment after your loan payments become due, notify your lender immediately. Sometimes, the lender can work out a repayment plan for you if you have an unusual hardship.

keep you busy for the majority of the time you work. To work in such a program, you must be eligible for federal work-study money, and you will be limited to a certain number of hours you can work per week. Not everyone who is eligible for work-study will be able to find a position on campus, however. Each department and area of the college advertises, hires, and manages work-study positions; sometimes, hiring can be competitive. There may be specific requirements (such as computer skills) that a candidate must meet before being hired. Because some positions require working with students' personal information, work-study students must also abide by the college's privacy standards.

The benefits of participating in work-study are that you can earn some money that will help pay your expenses and you will be able to work closely with college employees. By getting to know professors and administrators better—and by working for them—you may have access to valuable advice and information. To investigate whether work-study is available for you, talk with your financial aid officer. He or she will review your eligibility and help you apply for on-campus employment.

Tuition Waivers for Employees

Another source of financial help is your employer. Large corporations sometimes offer financial assistance for employees, although there may be stipulations that you work for a certain amount of time after graduation. If your employer doesn't offer scholarships to employees, you should still ask if he or she is interested in doing so; employers will benefit from employees who further their education. Finally, your college may offer tuition waivers for its full-time employees. Some students take jobs offered at colleges so that they can take classes for free or at a reduced cost. If you need a part-time or full-time job while you are in school, you may want to check out the openings at your community college.

Applying for Financial Aid

Each college is different in how it handles the application process, but it is worth talking generally about what to expect when applying for financial aid. Even if you have applied and received financial aid for this academic year, there may be some information that you need to know before applying again. The first step in the process is obtaining a Free Application for Federal Student Aid (FAFSA), which can be picked up from the financial aid office of your college or can be accessed online (http://www.fafsa.ed.gov/). Financial aid applications must be renewed each academic year; the time line for receiving aid for a year starts in August and ends in July. Thus, if you applied for financial aid in November and received it for classes that started in January, you will have until July to use that aid; then you will need to reapply for aid for the fall semester.

As part of the FAFSA application process, you will need to determine whether you are considered "independent" or "dependent." The federal government defines a student as being independent if he or she meets certain criteria such as being married, being born before 1981, or having both parents deceased. Students who fit the definition for dependent status, but who have extenuating circumstances, may be able to request that their status be changed to independent. In addition to determining your ability to pay for college, you will also be asked to provide an Estimated

Family Contribution (EFC) amount; for example, if you receive child support payments or Social Security payments, you will have to report that income as part of your EFC. One other consideration when applying for financial aid is that each year a certain percentage of loan applications get identified for verification. This means that student financial aid applications may take longer to process because of the requirements of verification.

Renewing Financial Aid and Paying It Back

In order to continue to receive financial aid, you will need to make sure that you understand and follow the requirements of your college. Many colleges maintain a satisfactory academic policy that states you will need to stay enrolled in a certain number of credit hours and maintain a certain grade point average to continue to receive grants and loans. Sometimes, the required GPA is higher than the GPA to remain in college. For example, you may have to maintain a 2.7 GPA to continue to receive financial aid, whereas you have to maintain a 2.0 GPA to stay in college. If you do not meet the requirements for a semester, your college may place you on financial aid probation, which means you must meet the college's requirements for the next semester to be removed from probation. The next step after probation can be suspension from financial aid. This means that you may not be able to receive financial aid, but you may still be able to enroll in classes as long as you pay for them yourself. Just in case your suspension is the result of extenuating circumstances, some colleges have an appeals process for financial aid suspension. This means you may file an appeal and appear before a group of people who will determine if you can reapply for financial aid.

Whenever you apply for loans, you will need to consider how you will pay them back after you complete your degree or when you stop attending college. Student loan default is a common problem nationwide, and there are stiff penalties for failing to pay back the federal government. On the other hand, loan forgiveness programs are often available for students who major in fields that are in high demand in their community. To find out more about these types of programs, be sure to talk to someone in the financial aid office at your college.

Creating a Budget

Whether or not you rely on financial aid to pay your tuition bills, creating a budget will help you meet your financial and personal goals. A budget doesn't have to be a headache. In fact, it is relatively easy to create a budget. The hard part is following it. First, you need to create a customized budget sheet. Table 2 shows a sample budget form that you can start with. In the first column, you will estimate your income and your expenses. The middle column will be used to record your actual amounts of income and expenses. Record any differences in the marked column by subtracting the actual amount from the estimated amount. For example, if you estimate that you earn about $1,000.00 a month, but this month, you earn $1,092.56, your difference is $92.56. If you earned $997.36, then the difference is −$2.64.

Once you determine the categories that fit your lifestyle, you will need to gather all the bills and paystubs that you have and add up your expenses and income. It is a good idea to review at least three months' worth of bills to get an accurate picture

TABLE 2   Sample Budget Form

Category	Estimated Amount per Month	Actual Amount per Month	Difference
Income			
Source 1 (wages/salary)			
Source 2 (scholarship, financial aid, etc.)			
Source 3 (alimony, employee tuition reimbursement, child support)			
Total Income			
Expenses			
Mortgage/rent			
Utilities			
Car payment/transportation			
Insurance			
Groceries			
Household items			
Clothing			
Gas			
Car maintenance			
Cell phone/pager			
Eating out			
Entertainment			
Health care (medications, doctor's visits, etc.)			
Credit cards or loans			
Total Expenses			
Net Income (Total Income minus Total Expenses)			

of your expenditures. If you have any bills that are paid less frequently than once a month, then you will need to convert them to a monthly expense. For example, if you pay $240 for car insurance every six months, your monthly expense is $40 ($240 divided by six months).

One key to an accurate budget that helps you track your spending is to be honest about your expenses. That means you must write down everything you spend, even the money you spend on snacks or supplies. You may find that you spend $25 a week ($100 a month) on items that are unnecessary. The more you can track unnecessary items, the better you can control your spending.

After you get an accurate picture of your income and expenses, you can start setting short-term and long-term financial goals. Because you are in college and probably trying to keep expenses to a minimum, you may think that creating and working toward financial goals will be a difficult undertaking until you have a job with a steady income and secure future. However, you can start setting small, short-term goals now. For example, your first short-term goal could be keeping a monthly budget and making adjustments periodically. Another short-term goal could be to gather all the documents about your financial aid and keep them organized until after you graduate. Meeting these two goals will help you reach larger goals down the road.

You should also write down your long-term financial goals. One of these goals could be financial freedom and security. However, in order to reach that long-term goal, you will need to make a list of other goals and start working toward them. Be sure to include in your long-term goals ones that prepare you for retirement and the unlikely event of disability and unemployment.

Credit Cards

Credit cards can be very tempting when you are in college because they are so easy to use and the offers pour in just about every day. The reality of credit cards, however, is that they can cause big financial problems, ones that are sometimes difficult to pay off. Think about this: You don't want to start a new career after college that pays a good salary only to send a substantial portion of it to a credit card company. While it may seem easy, try to avoid paying your college tuition with a credit card. The interest rate will be more than double (possibly even five times higher) than you can get with a student loan. Additionally, avoid as many unnecessary expenses as you can. Use the rule that if it is not vital to your life, then it can wait until you have the cash—even if it is a one-of-a-kind, super-duper deal.

In case you are still enticed to use a credit card, think about this sobering information. If you were to charge $1,000 on a credit card that charges 17% interest and you only pay $100 a month, you will be accruing more in interest than you will be paying each month. And that is only if you do not charge anything else!

Table 3 shows that paying twice as much—$200—each month for six months only reduces the balance by $276.21—after paying $1,200. Unfortunately, some students have many more thousands of dollars of credit card debt, and with

TABLE 3   Credit Card Payments

Month	Previous Balance	Interest	Balance + Interest	Payment	Remaining Balance
Month 1	$1,000	$170	$1,170	$200	$970
Month 2	$970	$164.90	$1,134.90	$200	$934.90
Month 3	$934.90	$158.93	$1,093.83	$200	$893.83
Month 4	$893.83	$151.91	$1,045.78	$200	$845.78
Month 5	$845.78	$143.78	$ 989.56	$200	$789.56
Month 6	$789.56	$134.23	$ 923.79	$200	$723.79

the current interest rates, it is no wonder that students can find themselves in an endless cycle of charging and paying minimums. If it is at all possible, put the cards away until you are out of college, and then use them wisely.

What if College Isn't for You?

There is tremendous pressure on those who do not have higher degrees to get them. Frequently high school students hear this pitch from parents, counselors, and teachers: Success in life depends on obtaining a college degree. People who have been in the workforce know, as well, that a college degree can be the difference between doing the same job until retirement and being promoted.

Critical Thinking

EXERCISE 4

What is your financial plan for paying for college? If you are receiving financial aid (grants, loans, tuition waivers, etc.), how is it enabling you to pay for the expenses of college?

PRACTICE

But does everyone need to go to college? College is a great place to continue your education and to make your career dreams a reality. There are also indirect benefits to pursuing higher education, such as improving your health and financial well-being because you know more about yourself and the world around you. Nonetheless, going to college is not the only key to success. There are many vibrant, intelligent, successful people who have not completed a college degree.

How will you know if college is not right for you? It may be difficult to tell, but you shouldn't quit going if you are unsure. The best way to discover how you feel about being in college is to ask yourself a series of questions. Then, talk about your responses with a college counselor, advisor, or trusted friend who can give you good advice.

* Who wants me to be in college?
* Do *I* want to be in college?
* How do I feel when I am in class?
* How do I feel when I am studying?
* How do I feel after I take an exam?
* What do I want to major in? Why?
* What do I want to do with my life? Do I need a college degree to do it?
* What do I value about higher education? What can it do for me?
* What is my passion?

Take your time answering these questions. You may find that your discomfort about being in college is really fear about a new beginning and the unknown. Being apprehensive about a new program or a new environment is perfectly normal and does not necessarily indicate that you are not right for college.

On the other hand, you may know very clearly that you do not want to be in college at this point in your life. College may not be right for you *right now,* which means that you should consider returning when you are certain it will be your top priority. Many people put off going or returning to college. One of the benefits of waiting is that when you return you will be more mature and more responsible, which means you will be more likely to complete your degree.

PLUS

(Personality + Learning Style = Understanding Situations)

Think about Juanita's dilemma regarding which instructor to take next semester and what degree plan to follow. Juanita is an independent learner and is usually shy. Because she still lives at home, although she is 18, she feels some obligation to consider her parents' opinions about her future. Using what you have learned from this chapter, what advice would you give her? How can she gain confidence in mapping her future for herself?

Now, considering your own learning style, personality type, and special circumstances, what would you do to choose the right classes, professors, and degree plan if you were unsure of what to take, from whom to take it, and how to choose the right major?

PROFILE

MY STORY
Learning Plan

Directions: Using what you have learned in this chapter and what you know about your learning preferences, choose a task or assignment that needs to be completed soon and create a learning plan that will help you accomplish this task. Then, write your *My Story* Summary, a one-sentence synopsis that crystallizes your newly created plan.

LEARNING TASK	
Time of Day	
Intake Preference	
Social Preference	
Task Management Preference	

MY STORY SUMMARY:

Path of Discovery

What degrees are you interested in pursuing?
Why do these degree plans appeal to you?

HOMEWORK

From College to University

Preparing for Unexpected Higher Costs

It is very likely that you will see a change in college costs when you transfer to a university. You may be paying twice as much for tuition at the four-year school as you did at your local community college. In addition to tuition, you may see added fees that you didn't have at your community college: fees for athletic facility use, sporting events, campus organizations, and labs are possible additional expenses. Be sure to read the college catalog carefully and add the fees to the cost per credit hour to get an accurate picture of what you will be spending per class.

Despite the increase in tuition and fees, you may notice that your bookstore expenses stay the same. Although the price of books can be a significant portion of your overall college expenses, it is unlikely that you will experience an increase in cost. However, upper-level science and computer classes require weighty textbooks and additional software. These books can cost as much as $100. Multiply that by four classes, and you will be paying at least $400 for the semester. An advantage, however, to transferring to a larger school is that there are more people from whom you can buy used books. Take notice of special discounts for used books in the bookstore and look for flyers on bulletin boards that announce books for sale.

From College to Career

The Benefits of Returning to Work Before Continuing Your Education

There may be a time when you must interrupt your college career to return to your job full-time. Balancing financial and educational goals may be too difficult to handle at the moment, which may mean that your financial needs take precedence. If this happens to you, there are some ways of dealing with the transition back to the world of work while still keeping your eye on returning to college.

First, realize that going back to work doesn't have to be forever. Just because you are unable to return for more than one semester doesn't mean you never will. Be sure to talk with your employer about your desire to get a degree. You may be surprised by his or her support of your goals. There may even be financial assistance for employees who take college classes. Remember to talk with your family and friends about your need to further your education as well. Someone may be willing to help you with finances, scheduling, and family duties. Set a time line for returning to college. If you need to work a semester to earn more money to pay for tuition, then be sure to keep up with registration periods and college announcements.

Finances will be another consideration, so be sure to save your money. Even if expenses were not the reason you returned to work, putting aside money in a "college fund" will make it easier to re-enroll in college. You won't have any excuses for not being able to afford the increased costs. Look for scholarships and financial aid for working adults. Some states are creating grant programs for nontraditional students who work full-time in order to increase the number of college graduates in their states. Finally, keep connected with former classmates and instructors. If you are aware of what is going on at the college, you are more likely to return because you will feel as though you had never left.

Chapter Review Questions

1. What activities will you participate in at the end of the semester and why are they important?
2. What should you consider when planning your degree?
3. What should you consider when you plan to transfer to another college or university?
4. What are the different methods of paying for college?

Case Scenarios

1. Anja is considering transferring to the university nearby after she graduates with her associate's degree. She is very nervous and is not sure what she needs to do to plan a successful move once she completes her degree. What advice would you give her about making the move and getting involved in the transition now?

2. Ramielle has paid for her first semester of tuition from her savings, but she is looking for other ways to pay for the rest of her college. She doesn't qualify for any grants and is not sure what her options are. Explain to her what choices she has to pay for college without incurring too much debt.

3. Riley has had a difficult time getting used to the expectations in college. He has not had a successful semester so far, and he is getting pressure at work to quit college and take a promotion. It means more money, but less time to get the degree that he wants. He could always come back, he knows, but at 25 years old, he is afraid that if he doesn't go to college now, it will be even harder when he earns a bigger paycheck. What would you tell him about quitting college?

Research It Further

1. As an individual, or within a group, research the qualifications and requirements for the different loans and grants that your college offers. With the information, create a one-page sheet for each type of financial aid that can help students remember the differences between each type.

2. Investigate the entrance requirements of two four-year universities in your area. Find out GPA requirements, available types of scholarships and financial aid, and what kinds of degree programs they offer. Make a brief presentation to your class.

3. What, if any, alumni services does your college offer? If they offer very few or none at all, brainstorm a list of ideas that you would like to see implemented and present them to an administrator at your institution who can give you feedback on what is possible. Then, report to your class on which suggestions can be implemented and which cannot.

Reference

U.S. Department of Education. (2008). Types of federal student aid. Retrieved 14 May 2008, from http://studentaid.ed.gov/students/publications/student_guide/2006–2007/english/typesofFSA_grants.htm

Understanding Others in College and Diversity

6

Understanding Others in College and Diversity

Candace Rowley/Merrill

Michael's Story

"Evan, are you going to be around later today? I may need some help," Michael asks his new friend and study group partner. Michael stayed after orientation to exchange numbers with Evan and, since then, they have talked a few times on campus and on the phone.

One reason Michael felt an instant connection with Evan that first day they met was that Evan is obviously different from him, someone who obviously has a different background, ideas, and experiences. From his experience in the military, Michael knows how to deal with diversity; he has met all kinds of people from different countries and backgrounds.

"Sure, man," Evan says. "Maybe you can help me, too. I have to move some furniture for my aunt this weekend. You think you can lend me a hand?"

Michael paces outside the library and drops his backpack on the wall before he sits down next to it. Although he has been through the college orientation, he is still getting used to the college experience. His philosophy professor, for example, has a very different view of the world and challenges her students to question their own views. Sometimes the debates get heated and he forgets that he is there to learn, not to get angry and shut down. His political science instructor does not agree with him on the responsibility and roles of state governments, but he does allow Michael to share his military experiences and is respectful of Michael's point of view.

"Are you sure you can use help from an old man like me?" Michael asks. Michael has never thought much about being 42 until some students he is working with on a group project said something about his being "too old" to work with.

"You may be old, man, but I'm pretty sure you can bench press more than me," Evan says as he laughs.

"Maybe when I was your age, but not anymore," Michael says. "Seriously, though, I have this group project, and, well, my group keeps meeting without me, and I have to get this project done or I am done for."

"Ah, c'mon," Evan says. "I would make you the leader of my group. I've heard you debate the professor before and win! You are fierce in an argument."

"I think that is part of the problem, too. I ran into a guy in the class and he said he saw two people in my group meeting in the library and working on the project when I was able to meet, but no one even called me," Michael says.

"So what do you need from me? Need some boxing tips?" Evan asks.

"Do you think if I talked to the professor that she would reassign me to another group or tell me to deal with it?" asks Michael.

"Man, what do you have to lose by asking?" Evan replies.

In This Chapter

One of the easiest parts of college can be the hardest for busy college students. The easy part to making friends and forging relationships is that people are everywhere—in class, computer labs, and the library—and everyone shares at least one thing, college, in common. As Michael will discover, getting to know those around you is essential to your well-being and happiness while you are working on your degree. The hard part, however, is making the time to cultivate relationships. As a community college student, you most likely have other activities that fill your schedule outside of class: work, family, hobbies, church, and friends. Part of this chapter's purpose is to show you the benefits of starting and maintaining strong relationships with people on campus.

In addition to making friends and connections with people in college, this chapter also discusses diversity as an issue to be explored and appreciated. You will certainly notice that the people you encounter in college are different and that you will most likely meet people who have different values, goals, opinions about politics and religion, and ways of leading their lives. An important component of being an educated individual is understanding that college is, in part, about learning to listen to others, understanding their points of view, and appreciating them in the larger context of humanity. This chapter, then, presents you with several categories of diversity—to be sure, there are as many categories as there are people—to explore and discuss with your instructor, classmates, and others. There is also discussion of instances in which a lack of appreciation for others' differences can lead to prejudging them, or worse, discrimination. All of these topics will help you create and maintain mutually respectful relationships with others and will help you broaden yourself and others in the world. More specifically, after reading this chapter, you will be able to:

* Describe the different types of people and their roles on your campus.

* List the benefits of cultivating relationships in college.

* Describe teaching types and how to learn from each type.

* Explain the importance of appreciating diversity.

* Discuss how stereotyping, prejudice, and discrimination are related.

The People on Your Campus

Research has shown that getting to know at least one person, no matter who it is, on your campus will increase the likelihood that you will stay in college and complete your degree. Whether it is the janitor or a career counselor, getting to know someone beyond just her name, title, and face is to your advantage while you are in college.

You have probably noticed already that there are many people who work at a college—and most of them are there to support and guide you through your college experience. Equally important to understanding where buildings and services are located is knowing who does what on your campus. It saves you time when you know, for example, that to get copies of your transcript will involve speaking with someone in the registrar's office or that checking on loan applications will include contact with a financial aid officer. All of these people are charged with the task of helping you succeed each semester you are in college, and it will make your transition from either high school or the world of work much easier if you are familiar with the various common jobs on campus.

Cultivating Relationships with Professors

There may be no one more important to your college and possible future career success than a professor. She does not just provide you with access to the content and support you as you think critically about the subject matter; she also can be a mentor and a resource as you complete your degree and start your career. One way to start out on the right path to a good relationship is to greet your professor with a smile and a "hello" when you see her in and out of class. College professors see their relationships with their students outside of class as part of their advising and mentoring duties. For many instructors, their students are not only people in their classes, but they are also potential graduates from their programs or transfer student success stories. Being friendly in and outside of class is a great way to start on the path to a strong, valuable relationship during your college career (and maybe even after!).

Another way to start developing meaningful relationships with your professors is to appreciate the diversity of disciplines, personality types, and teaching styles among them. For sure, you will not love every class (although we professors wish you could), every teaching style, and every personality that you will encounter in college. When you take pleasure in the class and the instructor, enjoy every minute of it; when you don't, use the experience to keep focused on what you want: a college degree. Also realize, however, that what you "don't like" at first may just be a first impression that will not necessarily be your feelings at the end of the course. Sometimes students' initial experiences in a class are uncomfortable, but those same experiences may be ones that they reflect on as the most meaningful because they learned something about the course topic as well as themselves.

Because each instructor's expectations in terms of class preparation and policies regarding attendance, late work, and make-up exams will differ, be mindful that rules that apply in one class may be different in another. Relationships built on acknowledgement of others' boundaries (in this case, professors' expectations and policies) as well as respect and integrity are stronger and more authentic. To cultivate a solid relationship with your professor, make the most of his office hours. Office hours are best used for questions about material that was previously covered, assignments and policies that were previously explained, and anything else that does not pertain to the day's lecture or in-class activity. Sometimes students only see office hours as a time to discuss a problem; office hours should be used for positive visits as well—stopping by to say "Hello!" or to follow up on an idea that sparked your interest in class are great ways to strengthen your relationship.

It would be a perfect world if there were no conflicts in your relationship with your instructor. However, there may be a time in your college career when you don't feel as though you have a strong, respectful relationship. If you experience conflict with a professor, be sure to discuss the issue as soon as possible—and in private. Use "I" statements to explain your perspective rather than "you" statements. For example, saying "I am confused about what our exam will cover" is better than saying "You were confusing when you talked about the exam." Using "I" statements also underscores your control over your actions and reactions during the conflict. Look, too, for common ground that can help you manage the conflict maturely and respectfully.

A good relationship for its own sake is perfectly acceptable, but also remember that professors can provide a link to other opportunities beyond the classroom. You will most likely turn to a professor when you need a recommendation letter for student activities, scholarships, internships, and jobs. Getting to know at least one professor well will give you an advantage when you want to move forward in your college career. Professors in your certificate and degree program are usually tied closely to the business and industry in which they teach. Thus, a good relationship with a professor in respiratory therapy, for example, may lead to a job opportunity in the field. A professor who teaches a general education course, one designed for transfer to a four-year university, may work closely with a professor in the same discipline at the local university. She may know about special scholarships or helpful people to contact once you have completed your degree.

Although a good relationship with your professor is a key to your enjoying your education experience, remember that your professor is not an equal in the relationship and still must challenge you to learn and stretch your concept of yourself and others, as well as evaluate you during and at the end of the term. Creating boundaries in relationships is discussed later in the chapter.

Getting to Know Advisors, Counselors, and Learning Support Staff

In addition to professors, some of the most important relationships that you will forge during college will be with people whose sole job is to make sure you succeed. Counselors and advisors will be key people in your academic career, so be sure to take the time to get to know these individuals. College administrators also play an important role.

Advisors. Your advisor may be the first person you encounter at college. An advisor explains to you what courses you should take, how many hours you should take a semester, and how to plan remaining semesters. An advisor works for you; it is his or her job to see that you complete your degree with little difficulty. You may be lucky enough to have the same advisor throughout your college career. In that case, regular contact with your advisor will help keep the lines of communication open. If you have a different advisor each semester, you may wish to find one person on whom you can rely to act as regular advisor. That person may be a former professor or a counselor who has advised you in the past. The goal is to find someone on campus who has an interest in your education beyond one semester.

Counselors. You should take the opportunity to get to know at least one counselor on your campus. Whether it is a career counselor or a disability counselor, make it a point to schedule an appointment with one while you are in college. Getting to know counselors is a great way to obtain more information about the school and its services. For example, a career counselor may inform you of a career fair or recruiting day. He can also help you prepare a resume and practice interviewing. Counselors who deal with students who have personal issues are another valuable resource for you. Even if you do not need personal counseling, you may benefit from a relationship with one. This type of counselor can give you tips for managing stress and dealing with difficult people, just to name a few experiences you may have in college.

Tutors, Mentors, and Student Leaders. In addition to the key people you will encounter in college, there are a variety of other people who work or volunteer their time to help you achieve your academic, career, and personal goals. Those people can include tutors in a learning assistance lab. Working one-on-one with them provides you with a unique relationship in that a tutor can really get to know what your learning needs are and how to help you fulfill them. A tutor can be a great resource for understanding the material for a class because he is often a student himself or has just recently taken the class.

Student or peer mentors are other types of people you will find on your college campus who can be instrumental in keeping you on track to success. Peer mentors are usually current students who have been successful in their classes and who are willing to provide support to new students who may need extra encouragement to navigate the choppy waters of the first few semesters. Peer mentors may give you advice for studying, for choosing a degree, or for balancing family, work, and college. And just think—if you are also successful, you may be a great peer mentor for a student who was just like you when you started!

One final group of people with whom you may come in contact is student leaders. You may find them in special clubs, associations, or student government. Unlike peer mentors, whose primary role is to work one-on-one with a student, student leaders work with both students and the college or organization to provide leadership in certain areas. For example, a student government representative may ask college officials to provide more family-friendly activities so that more students can attend with their children. If administrators agree, then the Student Government Association may work with students to find out what types of activities are best and may organize an event to get more students involved.

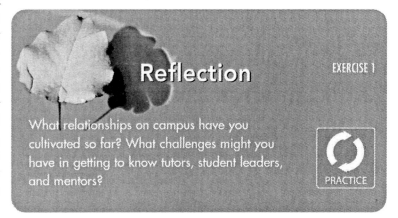

Reflection

EXERCISE 1

What relationships on campus have you cultivated so far? What challenges might you have in getting to know tutors, student leaders, and mentors?

PRACTICE

Getting Along with Classmates

Last, but certainly not least, getting to know your classmates can make the difference between struggling all alone and meeting new challenges with a like-minded support group. Who else can relate to the challenge of studying for a chemistry final exam than the students in the class with you? Think about it: Your classmates will be the majority of the people who populate a college campus. You may get to know well only three or four professors throughout your college career, but you have the potential of meeting and working with hundreds of students.

In addition to sharing experiences with your fellow students, you can also rely on them as study partners or emergency note-takers if you can't be in class. Another benefit to making friends with classmates is that you can learn about other classes, instructors, and degree programs from them. Their firsthand knowledge could help you choose the best classes and the most promising programs.

Getting to know your classmates can be relatively simple, especially since you will be sitting close to them during each class. Here are a few tips for creating lasting relationships with fellow students:

* Introduce yourself to those sitting around you. It may be easier to arrive early and start conversations with other students.

* Exchange phone numbers or email addresses with classmates who seem reliable and trustworthy. You may need to call someone if you miss class.

* Offer to study with someone. Not only will you help a classmate, but you will also help yourself learn the material.

* Keep in contact with friends even after the semester is over. While you may not share classes anymore, you still may be able to study and offer support to one another.

Creating Boundaries

Because you will be surrounded by a diverse group of people of all ages, it may be difficult for you to create and maintain the traditional boundaries that exist between students and their counselors, professors, administrators, and learning support staff. It almost seems contradictory, but boundaries may be necessary at the same time that you are getting to know others. Why should you refrain from close relationships with professors and advisors when you need them to get to know you if you are to ask for a referral or recommendation?

For one, some colleges discourage intimately personal relationships between professors and students, just as many companies prohibit the same type of overly friendly relationship between supervisors and their employees, because such relationships can be problematic. One possible problem is that intimate relationships can result in perceived or actual unfair evaluation or treatment. Because a professor is considered a superior, the college views the professor's role as one of authority and power. Many sexual harassment policies and laws are built on the imbalance of power between a person in authority and a subordinate.

Another possible problem is that other students may see the relationship as favoritism and feel as though they are being treated unfairly. Additionally, there is the possibility of a sexual relationship, which is sometimes strictly prohibited at colleges. If you have not already done so, check your student handbook regarding your college's policy about relationships between students and faculty. Ultimately, you will need to make the decision that is best for you and the situation as to how friendly you should be with faculty or other college officials.

If you get along well with your professor and genuinely enjoy her company, then your best move is to respect the professor–student relationship while you are in class. You can do this by meeting your professor during her office hours on campus and keeping conversations focused on your progress in your classes and your career plans. You can then continue the friendship after you have finished the semester and have no intentions of taking another class with that professor again. Some friendships between professors and students are long lasting, so consider cultivating them once the class is over.

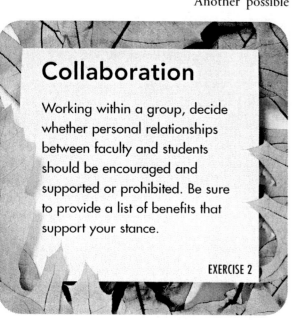

Collaboration

Working within a group, decide whether personal relationships between faculty and students should be encouraged and supported or prohibited. Be sure to provide a list of benefits that support your stance.

EXERCISE 2

When a Problem Arises

A time may arise when you have a problem in one of your classes. If it does, you can be assured that the college's employees will work with you to resolve it. There are, however, rules and procedures regarding how to resolve a problem at a college. Knowing and following these procedures will ensure that a problem is handled appropriately and quickly.

The first step to resolving a conflict in class is to define the problem. Is it a communication problem? Is it a problem with the course material? Is it a problem with the course standards? Once you have defined the problem, your next step is to discuss the problem with the person directly. If the problem is with your instructor, make an appointment during her office hours to discuss the issue. If you are emotional—angry, upset, nervous—wait until you have calmed down to discuss the problem. Your goal in meeting with the instructor is to resolve the conflict.

For the process of conflict resolution to work, you will need to complete the first two steps. If you are not satisfied with the result or if you feel the problem has gotten worse, not better, move to the next step: talking to the department chair or dean. You will no doubt be asked if you have met with the instructor. Again, your goal at this step is to resolve the issue. Occasionally, the instructor may be called in to help resolve the issue. Staying calm and focused on resolving the conflict will be to your advantage. In the event that the problem is not solved at this level, your last stop is with the dean of students or vice president for instruction. Starting at the top will only delay resolution.

Integrity in Relationships

Integrity is an important part of college life and the world at large. Integrity is defined as "a strict adherence to an ethical code of conduct," but the definition can be expanded to show its relevance to relationships. You can have integrity in relationships by being honest with other people and demanding honesty from them. Without integrity, relationships are superficial and meaningless.

The underlying factor of integrity in a relationship is trust. If you can trust others, then you will be better able to learn, grow, expand, and improve yourself. If you do not have trust, then you may shut yourself off from others and experiences that are new to you. Trusting others takes time—it isn't an overnight event. Give people reasons to trust you and then deliver on your promises. Likewise, put your trust in others, giving them an opportunity to prove themselves trustworthy.

A specific part of trust in relationships is reliability or, expressed another way, doing what you say you will do. If your classmate asks you to take notes for him on days he cannot be in class and you fail to do so each time, then you lack reliability. Your classmate will not be able to trust you to help him. If you agree to take notes knowing that you may not be able to do it, then you are not being honest—with him or yourself.

Acting with integrity is not easy and doesn't always come naturally. Instead, it is a conscious decision to do what is right even when it makes things harder and more uncomfortable for you and others. Being reliable and trustworthy takes more work because you may find yourself doing things (such as taking notes for a friend or driving a coworker home at the end of the day) that are inconvenient and time-consuming.

INTEGRITY MATTERS

Maintaining integrity in relationships includes being honest with others and with yourself. It takes time and energy as well as conscious decisions to be honest in order to build trust in relationships. However, the rewards are great!

Moreover, the rewards for acting with integrity are not always immediate; therefore, remember that despite how you feel at the time, the effects of your action will be far reaching and positive.

Tips for Lasting Relationships

As discussed at the beginning of the chapter, community college students do have a harder time cultivating friendships because of their busy schedules and because they do not typically spend four years with the same group of people. What else can you do to forge relationships in college?

Leave time in your schedule to talk with friends or meet with instructors. If you must leave directly after class to get to work, you will not be as successful in cultivating important relationships. One way to ensure that you connect with your professors is to make an appointment with them during the semester to ask questions or get feedback on your progress. Your ulterior motive is to cultivate a relationship with them. Also, be sure to approach conflict as an opportunity to learn more about yourself, and always act with integrity. Lasting relationships are ones that are built on trust and doing what is right.

Changes in Your Relationships with Family and Friends

Entering college will be a new experience not only for you, but also for your family and friends, especially if they have not gone to college. Communication, then, will be the key to weathering any changes in your relationships. They need to know how you feel about going to college, and they need to be aware that you will be going through changes while you are there. Surely you will be experiencing changes in your outlook on life, your belief in yourself, and your attitude toward the future.

When these changes occur, people around you may react differently. Some will be supportive and excited that you have created personal goals and are achieving them. A few, however, may react negatively. These people may be jealous of your success or your new "lease on life" because they did not have the same opportunities or because they squandered the opportunities that they did have. Others who react negatively may be insecure about themselves and feel "dumb" around a person in college; these same people often fear that once the college student graduates, he or she will leave them for a "better" spouse or friend. Also, there are parents who do not want to acknowledge that their children are grown adults who are and should be making decisions on their own; parents are also often worried that their children will be exposed to value systems and beliefs that are very different from what they taught them.

Whatever the reasons that the people around you react to the changes you experience, be comforted by the fact that you will survive, and better yet, you will have more of an understanding of the **diversity** of opinions that you will encounter. Learning how to deal with different people in college will allow you to apply what you learn to your personal relationships.

Exploring Diversity

An exciting part of college is that you will meet and work with people from all ages and backgrounds. Unlike a traditional university, at your community college you may be part of a study group that includes a grandparent, home-schooled teenager,

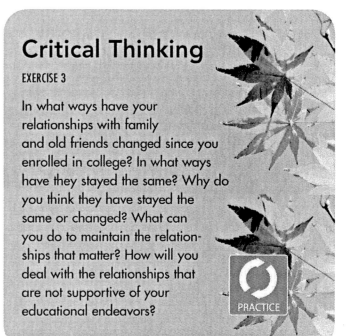

Critical Thinking

EXERCISE 3

In what ways have your relationships with family and old friends changed since you enrolled in college? In what ways have they stayed the same? Why do you think they have stayed the same or changed? What can you do to maintain the relationships that matter? How will you deal with the relationships that are not supportive of your educational endeavors?

PRACTICE

veteran, administrative assistant to a dean, full-time detective, and minister. At a community college, then, it is crucial to be sensitive to others' values and perspectives, which is one of the purposes of diversity.

A simple definition of diversity is "difference" or "variety." Another term heard when "diversity" is discussed in a college setting is "multiculturalism." Although the two words have different implications, they often have the same motivation—to expose the community to a variety of ideas, cultures, viewpoints, beliefs, and backgrounds.

When people talk about diversity, they usually mean race, gender, ethnicity, age, and religion. Colleges that want to promote diversity on their campuses often look for opportunities to hire and enroll people who have different backgrounds than the majority of the campus population. They do this with the belief that diversity enriches the educational experience for all because it exposes us, faculty, staff, and students, to new ideas and challenges our preconceived notions of the world around us.

Other Kinds of Diversity

Dealing successfully with diversity includes more than working well with people from different nations, different religious or political backgrounds, and different disabilities; you will also need to consider the diversity of attitudes and work ethics. For example, not everyone you meet in college or in your career will value the same things you do. What will you do if you work with others whose values conflict with your own? What will you do if the difference between your and others' work ethics cause conflict?

You will get the opportunity to work with others in class when you are assigned a group project or presentation. Even if you all are the same gender, race, religion, and age, you will still find that each of you is different and has different expectations

Lara Jo Regan/Getty Images, Inc.

The more you experience diversity, the more you will be able to appreciate the differences between you and others.

and opinions of the assignment. Being able to work with others, regardless of their learning and work styles, is a skill. The more you are exposed to diversity, the more you will be able to handle and appreciate the differences between you and everyone you meet.

Gender and Sexual Orientation Diversity

The latest educational statistics show that almost two-thirds of the college student population across the country is female. In the past few decades, women have enrolled in college in record numbers. It may seem strange to think that several decades ago, there were far fewer women in college, especially in law and medical schools. No doubt, you will encounter gender diversity at your college, and what this means for you is that you will have plenty of opportunities to work with both men and women and explore any preconceptions you may have about the differences between the sexes. You may have to pay more attention to society's assumptions about gender and be more attuned to how language, art, and sciences, among other disciplines, perpetuate gender stereotypes.

Sexual orientation is another type of diversity that you will more than likely encounter in college if you have not already. Homosexuality and bisexuality are just two categories of sexual orientation diversity. Organizations such as the Human Rights Campaign (www.hrc.org) strive to educate others about discrimination that can—and does—occur because of the stereotypes and prejudice that exist regarding sexual orientation. Why should you know more about sexual orientation as a part of diversity? Sexuality is part of the human experience, and one purpose of higher education is to help you better understand and appreciate your and others' human experience. Recognizing sexual orientation as a category of diversity gives you a more complete picture of humankind.

Sexual Harassment. Colleges and universities as well as the workforce have been aggressively educating students and employees about the definitions and prevention of sexual harassment for decades. Sexual harassment, by legal definition, refers to a superior, or a person in power, harassing a subordinate, or a person with less power than the harasser. College and employee policies often broaden the definition, however, to include any unwanted sexual advances that create an uncomfortable situation or hostile environment. This broader definition means that, in college, a student can sexually harass another student or a student can sexually harass a professor—or any other scenario that involves students, prospective students, and employees and guests of the college. To further round out the definition, women can sexually harass men and people of the same sex can experience sexual harassment.

Despite educational programs for new students and required seminars for employees, colleges—like any place in which people live and work—are not immune to instances of sexual harassment. According to Katz (2005), the American Psychological Association surveyed female graduate students about their experiences in college. The survey results found that 12.7% of female students experienced sexual harassment and 21% avoided taking certain classes for fear of being sexually harassed. Surveys about sexual harassment in the workplace paint a dimmer picture with 31% of female employees and 7% of male employees claiming to be sexually harassed at work.

Educating yourself about the seriousness of sexual harassment, your college's policy on sexual harassment, and the common behaviors that are often considered sexual harassment are steps in the right direction to minimizing incidents. For sure, sexual harassment is no laughing matter, and a review of your college's statement on the matter will reveal what lengths the college will go to discipline those who sexually harass others. Some college policies list the following behaviors as sexual harassment:

* Offensive jokes or comments of a sexual nature
* Requests or demands for sexual favors in return for favorable treatment or rewards (e.g., a good grade)
* Unwanted physical contact or assault
* Showing or distributing sexually explicit materials to others
* Posting sexually explicit images or websites in college-owned online course management systems or emailing those images or websites from college-owned computers

Although it may not be considered sexual harassment if it is not distributed to others, accessing sexually explicit websites with college-owned computer hardware and software may be prohibited conduct that will result in disciplinary action on the part of the college and possible criminal charges.

As with all forms of diversity and possible problems that can arise, be sensitive to others; treat everyone you meet on campus with respect; and be honest with others if you feel uncomfortable in a situation or with certain conversational topics.

Racial, Ethnic, and Cultural Diversity

Over the last 20 years, colleges embraced and developed multicultural studies in response to the past emphasis on "white, male, Western" history, ideas, and culture. Cultural and racial ignorance at its worst has led to the deaths of millions of people all over the world. Understanding and appreciation for the diversity in culture and ethnicity at its best create connections between peoples who have much to learn from each other. Table 1 provides you with activities that you can do to appreciate diversity.

Generational Diversity

The idea that our parents' generation is vastly different from our own, which will be greatly different from our children's generation, is considered a fact of life. One unifying viewpoint among the generations is that different generations view the world differently.

You will, no doubt, encounter generational diversity at your community college and in the world of work—more so than in generations past. The American Association of Community Colleges (2004) cites the following statistics from the National Center for Education Statistics: A 1999 study found that 46% of community college students are over the age of 25. Fifteen percent are over 40 years of age. These statistics mean that almost half of the students on a community college campus are not the traditional college age of 18–22.

What is a "generational cohort" and what does it mean for your college and work experience? According to Ron Zemke, Claire Raines, and Bob Filipczak, in their book *Generations at Work: Managing the Clash of Veterans, Boomers, Xers, and Nexters in Your Workplace* (2000), a generational cohort is a group of the population that was born within a certain period of time, that marked as important some of the same world events, and that hold certain common values. In their book, the authors recognize and

TABLE 1   Tips for Appreciating Racial, Ethnic, and Cultural Diversity

Work to eliminate all racial, ethnic, or cultural stereotypes or slurs from your thoughts and vocabulary. Stop yourself before you speak and ask, "Is this a stereotype or could it be offensive to some?"

Racial, ethnic, and cultural jokes, images, and cartoons are insensitive at best, harassment at worst. Avoid making fun of others' heritage. Be sensitive to others' backgrounds.

Learn more about your heritage and culture.

Strive to learn more about cultures that are new and different to you.

Participate in college and community cultural celebrations.

Attend seminars, guest lecturers, artistic performances about different cultures and countries.

Do not tolerate others who exhibit racial and cultural insensitivity. If you don't feel comfortable saying something to them, then avoid them and similar situations in the future.

TABLE 2 Generations, Birth Years, and Core Values

Generation	Birth Years	Core Values
Veterans	1922–1943	Dedication, sacrifice, patience, respect for authority
Baby Boomers	1943–1960	Health and wellness, optimism, personal growth
Generation Xers	1960–1980	Diversity, fun, self-reliance, global thinking
Nexters or Millenials	1980-present	Civic duty, morality, street smarts

describe four generations that can be found in the workplace (and college for that matter). These generations are defined and described in Table 2.

Each of the generational groups, the authors contend, holds certain values that influence how they work with others and how they achieve personal success. The diverse core values and attitudes can create enriching experiences for all generations that work together, or they can be a cause of conflict for those who do not understand and appreciate fellow students and coworkers of a different generation. Misunderstanding generational differences at its worst can become ageism, which is discriminating against someone because of his or her age. The key with generational diversity—as with all types of diversity—is to learn more about yourself and others and appreciate the differences.

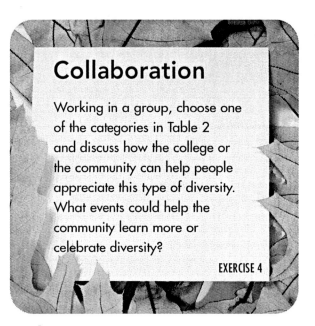

Collaboration

Working in a group, choose one of the categories in Table 2 and discuss how the college or the community can help people appreciate this type of diversity. What events could help the community learn more or celebrate diversity?

EXERCISE 4

Personality Types and Learning Styles Diversity

There are a variety of ways to describe what we are like and even how we learn. This information is certainly important in understanding ourselves, but it is also helpful as we work with others in the classroom and on the job.

Take, for example, a couple who is trying to decide what to do on Saturday night. One person suggests they go out with friends to a club to dance. The other person suggests they stay home and watch a movie. It's not hard to imagine that the subsequent conversation contains the question "Why do you always want to . . . ?" and either one person gives in and does what the other wants or each does what he or she wants to do on his or her own. Now, consider that the couple has taken a personality test and knows that one of them is an outgoing person and the other is shy. Knowing that each has a different preference when enjoying free time may not eliminate the conflict completely, but it does provide information and insight into the other's likes and dislikes. That information makes it easier for both to appreciate the differences and opens the door to compromise.

Now, consider personality types and diversity in the classroom or workplace. Exhibit 1 is an example of how personality diversity can affect group work.

Without knowing why the others are acting the way they do, do you think that this group will be successful in completing their task? Even if they do complete their

EXHIBIT 1   Example of Personalities at Play

Michael, Juanita, and Laura are working in a group to complete a task. Michael wants to list all the possible ideas before making a decision on which one they should pursue. Juanita wants to consider only one or two ideas because she feels that going through all of them would waste valuable time. When Juanita and Michael ask Laura which action they should take, she shrugs her shoulders and says, "I don't care. Whatever you want." Michael and Juanita are frustrated by Laura's reaction, because they assume she doesn't care about the project. Laura thinks both Michael and Juanita are wrong in their approach, but they are so domineering, she doesn't think it is worth telling them what she really thinks.

task, they will not be successful in understanding one another's work personality, which may cause problems later on if they are assigned to work together again. For sure, they will not understand themselves well enough to work well with other personality types on future projects. What if, instead of trying to work together without an appreciation for the diversity of personalities, they talk about what they are like and how they like to work? If Laura tells them that she avoids conflict and would rather listen to others than offer an opinion, then they will understand why she responds to what she thinks is impending conflict. If Michael tells the others that he enjoys generating ideas and needs constructive criticism in order to help him shape ideas, he may find that both Juanita and Laura would be more willing to give it to him. If Juanita tells them that she would rather support others toward a common goal rather than come up with the goal herself, the rest of the group may decide to reorganize how they are approaching the project in order to play on each other's personality types and strengths.

Teaching Styles Diversity

You will encounter many different personality types on campus, in and out of the classroom. You will also encounter a variety of teaching styles. It has been said that most professors teach the way they learn best, but there are college instructors who use a variety of teaching methods to encourage student learning. You will be more successful if you can identify each teaching style and what you need to do to adapt to it. Gone are the days of saying, "I just can't learn in her class. She doesn't teach the way I need her to." Like the people who must work together in groups and be sensitive to one another's personalities, you, too, will need to recognize what your learning style is and how it will fit into your professor's teaching style. Ideally, your instructor will recognize that his students have different learning style strengths and adapt his material to those learning styles, but not everyone you will encounter in college will vary his teaching style to meet your needs. Your best bet is to be ready to learn no matter what the teaching style.

To help you recognize the different methods of teaching, Table 3 contains a description of each and tips for making the most of the different types of classroom instruction.

TABLE 3   Teaching Styles

Teaching Style	Description	Tips for Success	VAK Category
Lecture	Professor talks for the majority of the class; a brief outline may be included; questions are limited or discouraged; usually very structured	Practice good listening skills; record lectures with permission; take good notes during class and review them frequently	Aural
Discussion	Professor poses a question and requires students to answer and build upon an idea or theme	Practice good listening skills; record theme or question for the discussion; note repeated ideas; record essence of each person's contribution; participate in discussion	Aural
Project	Professor bases class learning on projects; provides instruction for assignment; assigns roles; monitors progress	Make connection between project assignment and course objectives; ask for feedback during project to make sure you are progressing; refer to course materials for extra help	Aural, Kinesthetic
Problem solving	Professor poses or writes a problem on the board; walks through solving the problem	Break process down into steps; identify any step that is unclear; ask for extra practice and feedback if needed	Visual, Kinesthetic

Stereotypes

A discussion of diversity is not complete without mentioning some common problems. Stereotyping is an oversimplified opinion of someone or something. We often use stereotypes to make quick decisions every day. When choosing a checkout line, we may make a quick decision as to which is the fastest based on the people in line and what they have in their carts. When playing outfield on a softball team, we may stereotype the smaller players as weaker hitters, which will cause us to move closer to the infield. Parents also encourage children, who have difficulty making complex decisions, to stereotype strangers in order to protect them. Although these stereotypes are not necessarily harmful, they can create problems for us. We may get in a line we think will be shorter, but we end up standing in line for a longer time; we may move so close to the infield that the smaller player hits the ball over our heads; we may confuse children about the characteristics of a stranger, making it difficult for them to trust adults.

Stereotypes can serve a purpose in the short run, but as the examples above illustrate, stereotypes do not take into consideration all the facts. For the most part, stereotypes keep us from having to think about the complexity of issues, and often, then, we are unable to appreciate the beauty of diversity. In essence, stereotypes are a shorthand for evaluating situations and making decisions, but if used repeatedly, they can become prejudice and discrimination.

Prejudice

Prejudice is literally "pre-judging" a person or situation without knowing the facts. Prejudice is often based on stereotyping, which is one of the dangers of stereotyping in the first place. Let's take a seemingly harmless example of stereotyping that can result in prejudice: If you assume that all smaller softball players are weak hitters, then you may take that stereotype a bit further by disliking playing with smaller players because they don't make the game very challenging.

Like stereotyping, prejudice is a judgment based on little or no information or misinformation about a person or thing. In other words, it is based on ignorance or lack of correct information. That is why education is so important—you can avoid prejudging people and things by learning about them and making decisions about them based on *knowledge* rather than ignorance. Although we cannot always avoid stereotyping, we can eliminate prejudice and subsequently eradicate discrimination by making the decision to learn about others.

Types of Prejudice. As you have read above, there are a variety of ways we can categorize and classify ourselves and others. Used as one way of understanding ourselves better, these types of diversity are useful tools. If they are used to stereotype and then make judgments about people based on these stereotypes, then the categories become means to discrimination.

Sexist Attitudes. The increased numbers of women in college has changed the culture to be more sensitive and inclusive to women, but stereotypes and prejudice about females still exist. However, sexism is not limited to prejudice against women. Men, too, can suffer from sexist attitudes that are based on stereotypes. Examples of sexist attitudes in college:

* "My welding instructor is a woman! What does she know about welding? I can't possibly learn what I need to know for a job."
* "My male psychology professor is so much more demanding than the female professor. I should have taken her class instead. Plus, she would understand that I am a parent who has to juggle raising kids and going to school."

Homophobia. Sexual orientation prejudice is often in the form of homophobia, or fear of homosexuals. Homophobia is sometimes born out of ignorance of sexual orientation diversity, and sometimes it comes from a person's own background and values. Examples of homophobic attitudes in college:

* "My algebra instructor is gay. I don't approve of homosexuality, so it makes me very uncomfortable to be in his class."
* "I am avoiding taking composition so that I won't have to take the lesbian instructor who teaches it at the time I need it. She won't grade me fairly because I am a male."

Racist Attitudes. Racist attitudes can be obvious or subtle. People can hold racist views, like all other prejudices, and not realize that they are being intolerant of others. Asking people of other races what kinds of racism they experience is one way to understand what they perceive as prejudice. Monitoring your own words, actions, and attitudes is another way to be more sensitive to other races and cultures. You may think you don't mean any harm by what you say or do, but the recipients of racism don't always agree. Examples of racist attitudes in college:

* "I am going to study with the two Asian Americans in my physics class. They are super smart and maybe that will rub off on me."
* "The Hispanics at this college are only here to keep from being deported back to their own country. I resent having to take classes with them."

Ageist Attitudes. As you read earlier in the chapter, different generations have different values and viewpoints. An environment in which people from different generations work closely together can be exciting or tense, depending on how much people are willing to recognize, understand, and appreciate their generational differences. Problems arise, though, when people have prejudicial attitudes about a certain age group. We usually think of ageist attitudes as ones that stereotype people older than us, but people can hold prejudicial views against those younger than they. Examples of ageist attitudes in college:

* "I don't want to be in a study group with him. He could be my grandfather, and I am sure that he doesn't know one thing about computer networks."
* "I can't relate to the girls in my project group. All they talk about is going out and getting drunk. They have no real responsibilities and they don't take this class seriously."

Discrimination

Discrimination occurs when an action is taken on the basis of the prejudice. If, for instance, you decide that you do not want to play softball with teams with smaller players because you believe they are not as fun as teams with bigger players, then you have discriminated against smaller players and their teams. Because of recent laws and lawsuits, colleges and other places of business are sensitive to discrimination issues and spend a large amount of time and resources educating employees about it. Sexism, racism, and ageism are types of discrimination that are the most common in the workplace. It will be an important part of your education to understand how and why people discriminate so that you can avoid similar problems that stem from discrimination, which is why this chapter spends a considerable amount of time on this subject.

Even though most workplaces strive hard to eliminate sexual, racial, and age discrimination, there are still other types that can appear in everyday situations. For example, a coworker may declare that she won't hire anyone from a certain college because she believes that all its graduates are more interested in partying than working. Your boss may state his disdain for people from a certain part of the country and then refuse to promote an employee who is originally from the same area. Although you may not be able to change everyone's mind, you should be attuned to these more subtle, and sometimes acceptable, forms of discrimination and make an effort to eliminate them.

PLUS

(Personality + Learning Style = Understanding Situations)

Consider Michael's situation with his classmates. Although he is outspoken in class, confronting another person one-on-one is not his strength, and because he is not sure if his study group is shutting him out intentionally, he doesn't want to make the situation worse. He is also a visual learner, so what he sees or visualizes has a greater effect on him. Using what you have learned from this chapter, what advice would you give him? How can he combat the stereotypes that some in his group seem to have or that he has about others?

Now, considering your own learning style, personality type, and special circumstances, what would you do to resolve a conflict with your classmates in which you were required to work together on a project? How would you deal with any stereotyping, prejudging, or discrimination that may occur in the group?

MY STORY
Learning Plan

Directions: Using what you have learned in this chapter and what you know about your learning preferences, choose a task or assignment that needs to be completed soon and create a learning plan that will help you accomplish this task. Then, write your *My Story* Summary, a one-sentence synopsis that crystallizes your newly created plan.

LEARNING TASK	
Time of Day	
Intake Preference	
Social Preference	
Task Management Preference	

MY STORY SUMMARY:

Path of Discovery

Journal Entry

Reflect on how the information about diversity and relationships in this chapter has made you think about how you have treated others in the past. What mistakes have you made? What have you done well in terms of treating others with respect? What will you do in the future?

HOMEWORK

From College to University

The Relationships You Foster Now Will Open Doors after Transfer

Your relationships with advisors, counselors, and professors should yield more contacts at your new school. Advisors and counselors will be able to recommend certain programs and administrators. Professors will be able to put in a good word with the people they know at your transfer school, which may mean extra consideration for admission into a program or for a scholarship.

Those same relationships may also prove fruitful if your advisors, counselors, or professors have inside knowledge of little-known internships and aid, or if they know about deadline extensions and special transfer scholarships. The closer the relationships you have, the better able you will be to use your connections to make a smooth transfer. Advisors, counselors, and professors can also provide advice about the particular challenges you may face once you have completed the move.

From College to Career

Dealing with Diversity Is a Key to Success on the Job

We sometimes think that once we reach our ultimate educational goal and have started our dream career, we will be magically transported to a world in which everyone gets along. Unfortunately, we are brought back down from the clouds as early as the first day on the job.

Certainly, you will never stop needing to make positive connections with others or to redefine the relationships you already have. You will also encounter diversity on a daily basis and will have to rely on what you have learned in college (and life in general) in order to consider others' feelings, beliefs, and attitudes. What you have learned in college about other cultures, time periods, and philosophical and political ideas should provide you with a well-rounded view and will make it easier to work with and appreciate your diverse coworkers.

Chapter Review Questions

1. Name and explain four different categories of diversity.

2. How will you use what you have learned in this chapter to start and improve relationships with people on campus? Whom will you seek out and why?

3. What strategies can you use to deal with difficult people?

Case Scenarios

1. Jonathan has been raised in a very religious household. He believes that homosexuality is wrong, and he is struggling with an assignment in one of his classes in which he must write about the issue from a sociological perspective. The professor cautioned the students that they must be objective in their papers, but Jonathan doesn't think he can. What should Jonathan do?

2. Marie has been married for 14 years. She and her husband have twin girls who are 12. Since Marie started college, she has noticed that her husband seems less interested in her and what she is learning in her classes. He has started belittling her desire to earn a degree. Although he first encouraged her to enroll at the nearby community college branch in their town, he now seems to be against her continuing her education there. Marie has been discouraged by his reaction and is thinking about not enrolling next semester. What would you tell Marie to do?

3. One of Willis's professors has missed three night classes in a row without telling the students beforehand and without providing a plan to make up the missed material. Willis really needs this class for his major in business, and he is worried that he won't be successful in subsequent classes. He is also worried that if he complains to the instructor, his grade will be lowered in retaliation. Because he may have to take the professor again later, what should he do?

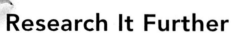

Research It Further

1. Review the section on teaching styles and determine what styles might be missing. Interview classmates in different courses to get ideas for other teaching styles. Write your own descriptions of the new styles and provide tips for being successful in those classes.

2. What does your college do to promote cultural appreciation on the campus? Collect examples of the college's promotion of multiculturalism and determine what, if anything, the college could do to enhance racial, ethnic, and cultural sensitivity and understanding.

3. What is your college's policy regarding relationships between students and faculty? In addition to reviewing your student handbook, interview students, faculty, and administrators about their opinions on the faculty-student relationship.

References

American Association of Community Colleges. (2004). Retrieved July 13, 2005, from www.aacc.nche.edu

Katz, N. (2005). Sexual harassment statistics in the workplace and in education. Retrieved July 5, 2005, from http://womenissues.about.com/cs/sexdiscrimination/a/sexharassstats.htm

Zemke, R., Raines, C., & Filipczak, B. (2000). *Generations at work: Managing the clash of veterans, boomers, xers, and nexters in your workplace.* New York: Amacom.

Handling Stress and Making Healthy Choices

7

Handling Stress and Making Healthy Choices

Evan's Story

Evan is a student by day and a kickboxer by night, usually competing several times a semester. At 20 years old, he can already tell that it takes him longer to see the results of regular strength training than it did three years ago. Even if he is a little slower in the ring, he has made up for it with smarter moves, the result of years of training both his body and his mind.

Because he is dedicated to the sport, he spends hours each afternoon and evening working as hard, or sometimes harder, than he does for his college classes. Sometimes he wonders if he can do both and be successful in and out of the ring. A few years ago, he saw a doctor because of depression, and he feels the symptoms creeping up on him again.

When he steps out of his car to enter the metal building that he calls his second home, a strong hand squeezes his shoulder.

"Evan, man, you're a little late today," his coach says. "What gives? You are usually early to practice."

"Hey, Coach. I hit some heavy traffic on the way in because I didn't leave at the time I usually do. Had too much homework to do," Evan replies.

"Evan, I know you are committed to college. That's great, but you have to do your time at the gym. If you don't, you won't be ready for your next fight. No offense, but I don't train second place."

The words sting Evan. He is highly competitive—you have to be, in this sport—and he prides himself on his athletic ability. True, he isn't getting any younger, but a winning title is still possible for an "old geezer" like him.

Then, there is college—another goal that he wants to achieve. When he registered for college, he really thought he could do both kickboxing and college and succeed at both. Most definitely, his workouts at the gym provide him with the energy release he needs. What better way to relieve stress and stay in shape than to box every day?

Evan packs his sweatshirt into his gym bag, stretches, and thinks about the homework he still has to complete before going to bed tonight, which will be around 2 a.m. if he gets home by 11:00. A few energy drinks and a protein bar will be needed to keep him awake to get his work done.

"I've got some extra drills we need to work on tonight," his coach says. "Can you stay another hour after you get your workout in?"

Evan hesitates. He has to finish a paper, and now he will need to stay up all night to get it done even though that will mean "sleepwalking" through his classes and maybe even his workout tomorrow.

"Sure, Coach," Evan says, and reassures himself that worrying about what he has to do won't make it any better.

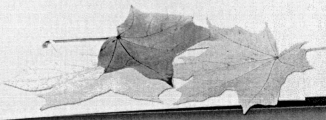

Chapter

us, minimizing the negative effects of stress and maximizing good health of making appropriate choices. How to decrease stress, how to improve , what to eat, how much to exercise, and how to reconnect with ourselves we make every day, yet so many of us make inappropriate choices. The make now are the ones that we will literally have to live with for decades We will be living longer than our ancestors did, but will our lives and our better? Some experts are seriously worried that we are making decisions health without thinking through the consequences.

purpose of this chapter is to provide you with information so that when you know better, you will make better choices for your physical, mental, and sexual health, which will in turn help you handle stress more effectively. Specifically, you will be able to do the following:

* Define stress and determine how to minimize its negative effects.

* Determine which health issues are important to consider while you are in college.

* Describe the kinds of stress-related illnesses and how to avoid them.

* Recognize the effects of drugs and alcohol.

* Identify methods to make better choices about your health.

Understanding Stress

Stress is a physical and psychological response to outside stimuli. In other words, just about anything that stimulates you can cause stress. Not all stress, however, is bad for you. For example, the stress you feel when you see someone get seriously hurt enables you to spring into action to help. For some students, the stress of an upcoming exam gives them the energy and focus to study. Without feeling a little stressed, these students might not feel the need to study at all.

Not everyone, however, handles stress the same way, and what is a stressful situation for you may not be for someone else. How we handle stress depends on our genetic makeup, past experiences, and the stress-reducing techniques that we know and practice. There are ways to reduce stress or change our reaction, both physically and psychologically. First, though, it is important to be able to identify causes of stress. The list in Table 1 is not exhaustive, but it can start you thinking about different ways that you experience stress.

TABLE 1 Possible Causes of Stress

Self-doubt	Pressure to succeed (from yourself or others)
Fear of failure or the unknown	Speaking in public
Congested traffic	Lack of support—financial, physical, or psychological
Uncomfortable situations	The demands of a job such as a promotion/demotion, deadlines, and evaluations
Life experiences such as the death of a loved one, having a child, getting married, and moving	Too many activities and not enough time to complete them
Waiting in lines	Computer problems

Stress Patterns

Each of us has certain triggers, such as the ones listed in Table 1, that stress us out. Usually, however, the same situation doesn't stress us out the same way each time we are in it. Take waiting in line at the bank. One day, you might be extremely angry to be waiting 15 minutes in a line to cash a check because you are late for a job interview. The next time that you are in the same line waiting the same amount of time, you may be calm and relaxed because you are enjoying a little quiet time to think while your mother waits in the car. Thus, it is not necessarily the situation or action that causes negative stress, but more likely other factors that are involved.

When you are suffering from lack of sleep, you may be more likely to react negatively to people and situations that usually would not bother you. When you are feeling unsure of your abilities to be successful in college, you may take constructive criticism as a personal attack. Being aware of times and situations that cause you the most stress is one step to helping manage stress better. If you realize that you are sensitive to others' feedback because you are feeling insecure, then you may be less likely to react negatively.

In Activity 1, place an "X" next to situations that are negatively stressful for you. Consider other situations or people that cause you to react negatively. The goal is to recognize a pattern of stress and then work to overcome it. When you are able to tell your professor or coworker that you experience negative stress when you are assigned a big project, then those who work with you or assign you a big project can help you create a plan to complete it.

ACTIVITY 1   Situations and Stress

SITUATION	STRESSES ME	DOES NOT STRESS ME
Starting a big project		
Paying bills		
Being in a messy environment		
Receiving graded papers and exams		
Not getting enough sleep		
Taking a personal or professional risk		
Getting out of bed		
Not getting feedback on my work		
Being distracted by other people		
Thinking about the future		
Taking tests		

Minimizing Stress in College

Because you will find stress in college, at work, and at home, it is important to be able to identify the different stressors in each environment and work toward minimizing the negative stress in each area. Some weeks, you will have to contend with negative stress in only one area, but there will be times when it seems as though each part of your life is making you miserable. The more you understand what you can and cannot control, the more likely you will be able to work through stressful times and stay on track with your goals.

Stress in college is inevitable, but it doesn't have to be overwhelming if you know what you can do to minimize negative stress in the first place. There are several ways that students unknowingly cause themselves stress: failing to read the catalog and student handbook about course prerequisites and descriptions as well as degree program requirements; registering for more hours than they can handle; trying to do too much at work and home; missing deadlines; arriving late for class or appointments; and keeping the same social schedule despite more academic demands.

The information in this chapter should help you minimize your stress in college by providing you with information and strategies for accomplishing your goals. Even if you avoid the above behaviors, you may still find that things don't go your way in college. If you realize that there will be times that you or others will make mistakes, then you will be more likely to bounce back from problems. Minimizing the negative effects of stress can include activities such as reading all information that you receive from the college; paying attention to flyers on doors, bulletin boards, and tables; and talking to your advisor, instructor, and counselor on a regular basis.

You will also want to regularly check the college's website for announcements and updates. Be sure, too, to read publications such as newspapers and newsletters that the college sends to the community. As always, ask questions when you are not sure of something, and make an effort to get involved with campus organizations and clubs because people in these groups often know what is going on around campus.

Minimizing Stress at Home

Reducing stress at home will, no doubt, be the first step for minimizing your overall stress. Because your family and friends are likely to be your most important supporters, what they think of you and the demands they place on you will need to be discussed. Some family members may be unsure of what you are doing or worried that your schoolwork will leave little time for them. Your friends may feel the same way, especially if they are used to hanging out with you after work and on the weekends. The key to minimizing stress at home is to communicate your needs. Talk to your loved ones about what you and they can expect when you are taking classes.

INTEGRITY MATTERS

One way to eliminate stress and anxiety is to make integrity a top priority. Even though it may seem less stressful to take the easier path, in the long run, your negative stress will be less when you maintain your integrity.

Some other tips for making your home life a sanctuary rather than an asylum include telling your family when you have exams or major projects due and informing them of your breaks and vacation time. They may be excited to count down the days until you are finished with the semester. Remember to explain how your responsibilities will change when you are in college. Also, be aware that you are a role model for your family—you may be inspiring other family members to go to college.

Minimizing Stress at Work

For some, stress on the job can be the most difficult to deal with because of the fear of performing poorly and being fired. Stress on the job can also be particularly tough to manage because you may feel uncomfortable confronting coworkers and being honest about your feelings. There are ways, though, to cope with the negative effects of stress at work. To help minimize the amount of stress that you have about your job, consider talking to your employer about your educational goals. Your boss may be very encouraging that you are increasing your knowledge and improving your skills. Your employer may allow you flextime to take classes, which means you may be able to arrive at work early, skip a lunch break, or stay late in order to take classes during the day.

As you would with your family, let your boss know when you have finals or other activities that may interfere with your regular workday, but avoid studying on the job. Be sure to handle any conflict that may arise from your schedule as soon as possible. Coworkers may be jealous of your success or they may misunderstand the arrangements you have made to work and go to school. If you have any concerns, address them to the appropriate person.

There is no cure-all for stress. It is an integral and important part of life and can actually be thrilling and exciting. Nonetheless, preventing it in the first place can keep you happier and healthier, which will make you better able to achieve your goals.

Reducing the Negative Effects of Stress

Because you cannot eliminate all stress, you will need to develop methods for reducing the negative effects that your body and mind experience when they are stressed out. One of the quickest, easiest ways to reduce the negative effects of stress is to take a deep breath. You may have even told someone who was upset to breathe deeply in order to calm down. The breath is, as many cultures have known for thousands of years, an important part of life; for example, in yoga, the ability to control the breath is essential to controlling the mind and body and to bringing fresh air to the lungs and other organs.

Visualization is another method for reducing the effect that stress has on the mind and body. In order to visualize a more relaxed time and place, all you need to do is to find a quiet, comfortable spot, sit down, and close your eyes. Relaxation experts suggest that you visualize a place that makes you feel warm and relaxed. Many people think about a beach because the mood there is often relaxed and the sound of the ocean is comforting. You will need to find your own special place.

Once you decide where you want to go mentally, you should start noticing the details in your place. If you are at the beach, then you should feel the sunshine's heat. Next, listen to the waves crashing on the surf and smell the salty air. Depending on how long you need to visualize this special place, you may want to stick your toe in the water or lie down on the beach and soak up the rays—leave your stress in those designated beach trash cans. The goal in this method of relaxation is to stay there as long as you need to; when you mentally return to your present location, you should feel refreshed and renewed.

Sometimes physical activity can be a better stress reliever than mental exercises. Getting outside or to the gym to work out your frustrations and stress is an excellent way of maintaining your health. By exercising, you can eliminate the physical side effects of stress while you take your mind off your troubles. If you do not usually exercise, take it slowly. Start with a 15-minute walk around the block or do some simple stretching exercises on the floor. Overdoing exercise can lead to more stress, so start small and increase the time you spend getting your blood circulating as you get stronger.

If you happen to exercise too much, you can look toward massage therapy to reduce all your stress. Although it is a little less conventional than other methods of reducing stress, a massage can improve circulation and alleviate muscle soreness. You can seek professional massage therapy or ask a family member to rub your neck, shoulders, or feet. Massage therapy can give you the rejuvenation you need to tackle the rest of the week.

You have heard the cliché that "Laughter is the best medicine," and it is also an ideal way to eliminate stress. Have you ever been in a very stressful situation when someone made you laugh and you thought, "Boy, I needed that"? You probably felt all the tension melt away as you doubled over giggling. Surrounding yourself with people who make you laugh is one way to keep stress at a minimum. Other ways include renting comedies or reading funny books. Of course, good, old-fashioned acting silly can relieve stress and anxiety as well.

Last, you can comfort yourself with familiar favorites to eliminate the negative effects of stress. A special meal or a visit with your best friend can put you at ease. Looking at old photographs, reminiscing about family trips, and watching your favorite movies can be great stress relievers. If you have enrolled in college in a new town or you have moved out on your own for the first time, you may find comfort in the familiar, whether it be an old pillow or a favorite movie. Make sure, though, that your methods of reducing negative stress are healthy. Drugs and alcohol may temporarily relieve stress, but they cause more problems in the long run.

Staying Flexible

An important method of managing stress is to remain flexible. If you try to control too many aspects of your life, you will quickly discover you can't do it all. Although it is important to manage your time and mark your progress toward your goals, you still need to plan for the unexpected and be willing to make adjustments. Good time managers plan for problems by keeping their schedules loose enough to make room for adjustments. For example, if you have a doctor's appointment at 2:00, you shouldn't schedule a job interview at 3:00. Delays in the doctor's office or traffic problems could keep you from your 3:00 appointment and cause more stress, just like with Evan. Instead, you should give yourself plenty of time in between scheduled tasks, especially if you will have to rely on others' time management skills.

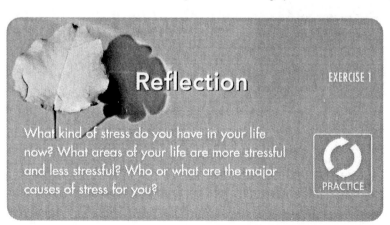

Reflection   EXERCISE 1

What kind of stress do you have in your life now? What areas of your life are more stressful and less stressful? Who or what are the major causes of stress for you?

PRACTICE

Knowing When to Get Help with Stress

If you ever feel as though you cannot cope with the amount of work and responsibility that you have—despite attempts to reduce your stress—seek professional help. Excessive crying, difficulty breathing, inability to get out of bed, and suicidal thoughts are severe reactions to stress. Knowing when to reach out to other people will be crucial in your recovery.

When asking for help, find someone you trust and who will be objective about your experiences. Sometimes, close friends and family members can be your best allies to combat stress, but other times an outside party, who will listen to what you have to say without judging, can be extremely helpful. When you talk to someone, be honest about what you are feeling. Don't try to minimize any fear or anxiety. The more the person knows about what you are experiencing, the better able he or she will be to help.

What's Good for You

Think about this scenario: You have just bought a brand-new car and you are about to drive it off the lot. Before you do, the salesperson provides you with an owner's manual and begins to tell you how often you will need to fill the tank, replace the oil, check the brakes, and rotate the tires. You tell the salesperson you don't need to know any of that stuff, and you drive the car off the lot. Besides, you know that the car needs to be filled up whenever the light on the dashboard comes on. What else is there to know?

For those who own and drive cars, you can imagine what will happen next. One day, maybe in a few months or a few years, you will find the car stops working regularly or stops working at all. In some cases, the repairs are minimal; in other cases, major repairs must be made to get the car into shape. The costs could be astronomical, so much so that you find yourself without a car and without hope for getting another one any time soon.

Now, consider that the car is your body. You know when you are hungry and when you are tired, when you feel happy and when you are stressed, but do you know how to take care of yourself? Maybe you do know that exercising will improve your health and help you manage your stress, but you won't make the time to include fitness as a part of your weekly routine. Just as a car may drive well for a while without regularly scheduled maintenance, there will come a day that the neglect will keep it from running properly or at all.

Learning to take care of your physical and mental health is crucial to getting where you want to go. To continue the car analogy, you won't be arriving at your destination if the vehicle is not in proper working order. One of the benefits of higher education is that you learn to make better choices, and that includes making better choices about your health. You can do that by understanding what you can control and how to get information to stay physically and mentally healthy.

Healthy Eating

One key to living a healthy life is making it a priority to eat nutritious food. Getting the recommended daily allowances of fruits, vegetables, whole grains, proteins, and fats is a commonsense approach to healthy eating, but as a society, we are choosing less healthy foods that are quick and easy—and loaded with calories, fat, salt, and sugar. Some of the reasons for poor nutritional choices include lack of time, information, and access to healthy alternatives. Increased stress is another reason that students make poor food choices; they may choose comfort food over nutritious alternatives.

To make healthier choices, arm yourself with information. As with any aspect of your health, the more you know, the better choices you can make. Learn what healthy foods are and seek them out. Read about and pay attention to serving sizes; too much of even a healthy food can add unneeded calories and contribute to weight gain. Read and learn to interpret food labels and ingredient lists that provide information about what is in the food and how much of it represents recommended daily values. The U.S. Food and Drug Administration (2004) provides detailed information on their Web page "How to Understand and Use the Nutrition Facts Label," which can be accessed at http://www.cfsan.fda.gov/~dms/foodlab.html.

Another way of getting nutritional information is to talk with a physician or a nutritionist to get a better idea of what kinds of food will be best for you to consume. Regular doctor visits will determine if you have any potential health risks, such as high blood pressure or diabetes, which will make your food decisions even more crucial to good health. Keeping chronic illnesses in check with monitoring and medication will not only help you feel better, but it will also keep you healthy for the long term.

Eating healthy means eating regularly. Most experts recommend eating smaller meals more frequently rather than heavy meals 5–7 hours apart. At the very least, as nutritionists recommend, start the day with a healthy breakfast, even if you don't have enough time to sit down and eat a full meal. You will feel more alert and energized throughout the early morning. However, what you eat for breakfast is just as important as eating something. Powdered doughnuts and a sugary, caffeinated soda will not provide you with the nutrients you need to be at your best. A piece of fruit and a cup of yogurt, for example, would be a better choice if you have to eat on the run. In addition to smaller, frequent nutritious meals, drinking plenty of water throughout the day has numerous health benefits, including regulating body temperature and assisting digestion.

Avoiding fad diets is another strategy for staying healthy. Although they may promise increased energy and weight loss, the results may be short lived and potentially harmful. A better approach to eating healthy is to stick to the recommended guidelines from the Food and Drug Administration or a health expert. Be aware, too, of the potential for eating disorders such as anorexia and bulimia. Anorexia, a condition in which people strictly control how much food they eat, and bulimia, a condition in which people cycle between overeating (binge-eating) in a short amount of time and then purging (through vomiting or abusing laxatives), are two eating disorders that can cause serious physical and psychological harm. Students who suffer from anorexia or bulimia, or believe they do, should see a health professional as soon as possible.

Why should you be concerned about what you eat and how much? One benefit of eating healthy is that it improves your body's functions. You may find that eating better improves your ability to sleep or reduces the fatigue you feel by the end of the day. Eating well also improves your mental abilities. Studies have shown that eating certain foods, such as fish, can improve your test-taking abilities. Finally, healthy eating and avoiding overeating helps keep stress under control, which in turn keeps stress-related illnesses at a minimum.

TIPS FOR HEALTHY EATING IN COLLEGE

* Find and read reliable information about health issues.
* Eat consciously and take time to appreciate the nourishment you are receiving from healthy foods.
* Plan your meals *and* snacks ahead of time so that you are not susceptible to last-minute, poor choices.
* Take bottled water in your backpack and drink it throughout the day.
* Take healthy snacks with you to eat between classes to avoid making unhealthy choices at the vending machines or at the student union.
* Pay attention to serving sizes and eat what you need to stay healthy, not the amount that you want to eat.
* Make wise choices at vending machines by avoiding food that is high in fat, caffeine, sugar, or salt content.
* Make any changes gradually. Think long-term health, not short-term results.

Exercise

We all know that making good choices about nutrition and exercise are part of a healthy lifestyle, but busy students often find it difficult to squeeze in time to work out. Take into consideration that as a student, you will spend many hours sitting down studying or working on the computer. Even if you have had a regular exercise routine, you may find that you have to make studying a higher priority.

Because you may have less time for exercise, it will be even more important that you find time to include some exercise in your busy schedule because of the numerous health benefits. At the very least, getting regular exercise will help you relieve stress.

Regular exercise can lower blood pressure, increase your metabolism, improve muscle tone, and lessen your chances of suffering diseases that are directly related to a sedentary lifestyle. It can also improve your mood and your self-confidence. Experts vary on how much exercise is ideal, but most agree 30 minutes of sustained activity three or four times a week will provide you with health benefits.

If you have trouble getting started or staying in an exercise routine, consider setting fitness goals that are reasonable and achievable. Reward yourself whenever you meet your goals, and don't get discouraged if you fall short now and then. Exercising regularly should be a lifestyle, not a short-term activity, so think of your progress as part of a long-term plan to live better. As with any exercise program, see a doctor before you begin and start gradually if you are not usually physically active.

TIPS FOR EXERCISING IN COLLEGE

* Take a physical education class at your college.
* Use the exercise facilities and equipment on your campus.
* Take advantage of walking trails or paved walkways on your campus.
* Park farther away from the buildings and get extra steps in.
* Join a gym and go regularly.
* Ask a friend to exercise with you.
* Incorporate short sessions of exercise into your studying routine by taking walking or stretching breaks in between reading or writing papers.
* Learn how to play a new sport or investigate a new form of exercise.

Getting Enough Sleep

Getting an adequate amount of sleep each night is as important to maintaining good health as what you eat and how often you exercise, but most Americans, especially college students, do not get enough sleep to maintain their health. Experts say that adults should get 7–9 hours of sleep a night to function normally throughout the day, but millions regularly get 6 hours or less. While you are in college, you may believe that 6 hours a night sounds like a luxury as you juggle your multiple responsibilities. For sure, there will be times that, because of circumstances, you will not be able to get enough sleep, but those times should be few and far between. Maintaining a regular schedule of going to bed and getting up will help you get the amount of sleep you need. Despite the myth of what college life is like, pulling "all-nighters" to study for tests or complete assignments is strongly discouraged, because it will make you less likely to perform well the next day.

For some students, the idea of keeping a regular sleeping and waking schedule seems impossible because of other factors that limit their ability to sleep. The reasons for many students' sleep deprivation are varied, but include health problems such as breathing obstructions and stress. If you believe your lack of sleep is the result of medical problems, consider seeing a health care professional. For stress-related sleep problems, practicing stress-relieving strategies will help alleviate the symptoms; however, if you find that relaxation techniques do not improve your ability to sleep well, then consider seeing a general practitioner or mental health professional for issues regarding stress.

What you put into your body can affect your sleeping habits. Eating high-fat and high-sugar foods near bedtime can slow you down, even if they seem to speed you up at first. Good sleep can also elude you if you consume alcohol and caffeine—even in small amounts—close to the time that you go to bed. Drugs, including medications for common illnesses, can deprive you of sleep or make you feel sluggish after you take them. Avoid consuming food, drink, or medications that overstimulate or make you drowsy right before bedtime. Never abuse prescription, over-the-counter medication, or illegal drugs to stay awake.

In addition to what you put into your body, what you do to it will affect your ability to get a good night's rest. Exercising too close to your bedtime will make it harder to fall asleep. However, too little physical exertion during the day can also contribute to difficulty falling and staying asleep. Experts suggest exercising early in the day—an activity as easy as walking for 30 minutes will suffice—in order to sleep more productively at night. Regular exercise will also help you alleviate the negative effects of stress. If you find, though, that you cannot "shut off" your mind because thoughts overwhelm you, consider writing down your worries—anything you may stay up thinking about after the light is off—in a journal, which will help you unwind and put away your day's thoughts.

Because sleep deprivation can contribute to irritability, depression, and physical health problems, it is important to make getting enough sleep a priority throughout the semester. If you have difficulty sticking to a regular sleep schedule, treat it like any other goal and write down what you want to do. Make it easier to achieve your goal by keeping your bed and bedroom free of clutter and by avoiding using your bed as a place to do homework or watch television. In other words, creating a sanctuary in your bedroom, a place where you can truly relax, may alleviate stress and anxiety that contribute to sleeplessness. Finally, avoid taking naps during the day, even on weekends, because they can throw off your sleep schedule. If you have an irregular schedule because of working different hours each day of the week, find a system that is relatively regular and that works for you. You may have to be creative about how you get enough sleep each evening or day.

The bottom line is that sleep deprivation can be dangerous and deadly. How little sleep you get should not be a medal of honor that demonstrates how much you work or how dedicated you are to meeting your goals. Getting enough sleep is a necessary part of living well, enjoying what you *do* accomplish, and being enjoyable to be around when you are awake.

Stress-Related Illnesses

Stress can cause a variety of health-related problems, and as you read above, sleep deprivation is one of those issues. Stress-related illnesses can vary from person to person, but there is one common denominator: With information and techniques for reducing stress, you can decrease the negative health effects. Although some of the following illnesses can be caused by other factors such as heredity and environment, they can be signs that stress is making you ill:

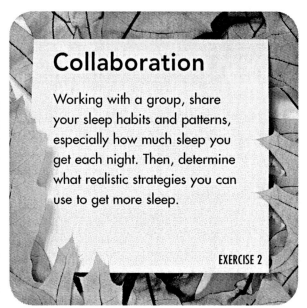

Collaboration

Working with a group, share your sleep habits and patterns, especially how much sleep you get each night. Then, determine what realistic strategies you can use to get more sleep.

EXERCISE 2

* Digestive problems including upset stomach, heartburn, constipation, diarrhea, and ulcers
* Severe headaches and migraines
* High blood pressure, heart attack, and stroke
* Muscle and joint pain
* Cold, flu, respiratory, and sinus infections

Staying healthy by eating well, exercising, and getting adequate sleep are all ways to help prevent stress-related illnesses. Be careful, especially at stressful times such as the beginning and end of the semester, that you do not neglect both your physical and mental health, for you will be more susceptible to stress-related illnesses that could keep you from doing well in college.

Drugs and Alcohol

There are some habits that we know are potentially hazardous to our health, and yet some people still do them. Smoking and using tobacco products, taking drugs, and consuming too much alcohol are known risks, but college students sometimes pick up these poor health habits because of peer pressure, a desire to fit in, and a need to find a way to relax or escape.

According to the American Heart Association (2008), about a quarter of Americans smoke, and people with the least education (9–11 years in school) are more likely to smoke than people with more education (more than 16 years in school). Smoking or chewing tobacco carries with it increased risks of heart disease, stroke, high blood pressure, cancer, and emphysema. The more educated you become about the health risks that are associated with smoking and using smokeless tobacco, the more it will be obvious that using tobacco products can cause serious health consequences. There are a variety of methods for quitting. It is worth investigating what your college and community offers if you are a smoker or a user of smokeless tobacco. Your college may provide information, support groups, or physician referrals for students who want to quit.

Alcohol and drugs are two other health issues that affect college students—sometimes even before they get to college. Having parents, partners, or friends who have abused drugs or alcohol is one way students can be affected. They may feel that they have to take care of others who drink too much or take drugs, which can take a toll on their time and emotional well-being. Students may also suffer from abusing drugs and alcohol while in college—and the effects can be far reaching. According to Facts on Tap (2008), a website that offers drug and alcohol education and prevention information, 159,000 first-year college students will drop out of college because of issues related to drug and alcohol abuse.

Being drunk or high can have grave consequences, the least of which is that you will do something you later regret. You increase your risk of having an unwanted sexual experience and causing physical harm to yourself and others. Death from overdosing on drugs and alcohol can happen even for those who are first-time users. Whether they are consumed for recreational purposes or because of other, more serious health reasons, abusing drugs and alcohol should not be a part of your college career because you will find it more difficult to reach your educational and personal goals.

In addition to abusing alcohol and illegal substances, using medications for purposes other than for what they were prescribed can have grave consequences, including death. Excessive use of medications that contain amphetamines and narcotics may seem like a good idea at first if you have trouble staying awake or going to sleep, but using them for a longer period than they have been prescribed can lead to dependency.

TIPS FOR AVOIDING DRUGS AND ALCOHOL IN COLLEGE

- Educate yourself about the effects of abusing drugs and alcohol.
- Cultivate relationships with people who have healthy habits.
- Avoid situations in which you know drugs and alcohol will be present.
- Take walking breaks instead of smoking breaks.
- Find other ways to relax that are healthy, free, and legal.
- Talk with a counselor or health care professional if you feel you are about to make a poor decision regarding the use of drugs and alcohol.
- Appeal to your vanity, if all else fails: Drugs, alcohol and tobacco make you look and smell bad.

Depression and Suicide

The pressures to succeed and juggle multiple priorities can lead to negative stress and feelings of being overwhelmed. Many times, feeling a little stressed during the semester is normal, but there are times that students can feel as though they are in over their heads, with no hope of getting out. It is no wonder that one of the most common mental health issues on college campus is depression.

In an online article about college students and depression, Neil Schoenherr (2004) reports that Alan Glass, M.D., the director of student health and counseling at Washington University–St. Louis, claims problems students face often start before they enroll in college: "Students arrive already having started various medications for depression, anxiety and attention deficit disorders." Signs of depression include loss of pleasure in activities, feelings of hopelessness, inability to get out of bed, increased use of alcohol or drugs, changes in appetite or weight gain or loss, changes in sleep patterns (sleeping too little or too much), extreme sensitivity, excessive crying, lack of energy or interest in participating in activities, and lack of interest in taking care of oneself.

Suicide is another mental health issue that is associated with depression. With the startling statistic that 25% of college students have contemplated suicide, it is no wonder that college health and counseling centers strive to educate students about the signs of severe depression and potential suicide attempts. Thoughts of ending your life should always be taken seriously and you should seek help immediately. Call a college counselor, an advisor, a hospital emergency room, or 911 if you are thinking about committing suicide.

Sexual Health Issues

A discussion of health issues would not be complete without talking about sexual health. Most colleges and universities strive to educate their students, especially those who are recently out of high school, about sexual responsibility and common sexually transmitted diseases (STDs).

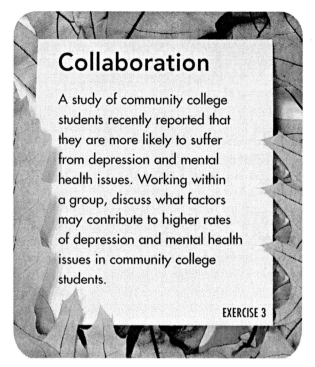

Collaboration

A study of community college students recently reported that they are more likely to suffer from depression and mental health issues. Working within a group, discuss what factors may contribute to higher rates of depression and mental health issues in community college students.

EXERCISE 3

Gary Gately (2003) reports that many experts and college officials have been alarmed at the recent statistics that show 73% of students report having unprotected sex while they are in college. More disturbing is that 68% of those having unprotected sex do not consider themselves at risk (Gately, 2003). This last statistic points to a major reason why students, despite sex education in high school or elsewhere, continue to engage in risky sexual behavior: Students, especially those 18–24 years of age, believe they are immortal and that nothing they do will have negative consequences. Because most STDs lack immediate visible or physiological symptoms, students who are at risk for contracting a sexually transmitted disease rarely ask to be screened for signs of infection.

Risky behavior, which includes having sex with multiple partners and having unprotected sex, opens the door to possible infections and illnesses such as chlamydia, gonorrhea, genital herpes, HIV, and AIDS (see Table 2). Some diseases can be transmitted in ways other than sexual intercourse. Hepatitis B and C are both diseases that can be contracted through shared razors, toothbrushes, body piercing, and tattooing.

TABLE 2 Common Sexually Transmitted Diseases

STD	Symptoms	Treatment
HIV and AIDS	May have no symptoms; extreme fatigue, rapid weight loss	No cure, but prescribed medication can keep the virus from replicating
Chlamydia	May have no symptoms; abnormal discharge, burning during urination	Antibiotics
Genital herpes	May have no symptoms; itching, burning, bumps in the genital area	No cure, but prescribed medication can help treat outbreaks
Gonorrhea	Pain or burning during urination; yellowish or bloody discharge; men may have no symptoms	Antibiotics
Hepatitis B	Headache, muscle ache, fatigue, low-grade fever, skin and whites of eyes with yellowish tint	No cure, but prescribed medication can help guard against liver damage

If you are sexually active, it is important to be screened regularly for STDs even if you do not have symptoms. Your long-term health and the health of those you come in contact with are at risk if you do not. As with any health issue, educate yourself with the facts about risk factors and symptoms. Then, monitor your behavior, practice safe sex, and see a doctor regularly to maintain good health.

Healthy Relationships

Maintaining healthy relationships are as much a part of your good health as eating nutritious foods and exercising. Some issues are signs of unhealthy, even dangerous, relationships. One type of unhealthy relationship issue is abuse: physical, mental, verbal, and sexual. Being in a relationship with someone who is abusive is not healthy. Although the previous statement seems like common sense, take time to think about it. No one deserves to be hit, controlled, or humiliated, *ever*.

Although we know that someone who makes us feel bad physically or emotionally can prevent us from being our best, studies find that abused men and women find it difficult to get out of abusive relationships. One reason people stay with abusive partners is that the abusers are—at first—charming, attentive, and loving. Usually, abusers begin to show subtle signs that something is not right; they may be extremely jealous, verbally insulting, and focused on your every move. Victims may also be dependent financially or emotionally on their abusers, which makes eliminating their influence difficult at best.

One particular type of unhealthy relationship that occurs most frequently among traditional college students is date or acquaintance rape. Simply defined, date rape is a forced sexual act in which one party does not actively consent; often, the two people involved are not complete strangers—hence the terms "date rape" and "acquaintance rape." Both men and women can be victims of date rape, although women are more often victims. Alcohol or a "date rape" drug such as Rohypnol may be involved in the incident. Many experts warn college-age women and men about the risk factors for date rape and encourage them to get to know whom they are going out with, not getting intoxicated, making sure their food or drinks are not handled by others, and communicating loud and clear if they find themselves in an uncomfortable situation.

Maintaining a healthy relationship takes time and energy, but there are many ways to make sure your relationships are positive experiences. For example, get to know people well before spending time alone with them. Learn to communicate your wants and needs effectively. Say "no" loud and clear when you do not want something to happen. Watch for signs of abusive and controlling people; sometimes, people show you signs of their true selves in smaller, subtler ways early in a relationship. If a situation makes you uncomfortable, get out of it immediately. Last but not least, do not abuse alcohol and drugs, which can impair your ability to judge situations. If you feel as though you have no options in removing yourself from an abusive relationship, seek professional help.

Communication Challenges

Sometimes one of the most important activities that promote good mental health is communication. Keeping feelings bottled up inside can lead to unhealthy thoughts and expectations. Learning to express fear, anger, and disappointment can have the effect of lessening the negative stress from carrying those feelings bottled up inside. If you do not feel comfortable saying what is on your mind to family and friends, you may start by talking with a counselor or therapist who can help you learn to communicate more openly with others. You can also learn effective communication techniques as well as conflict management methods that will help you deal more successfully with strong feelings by reading books and articles and watching others who model effective behavior.

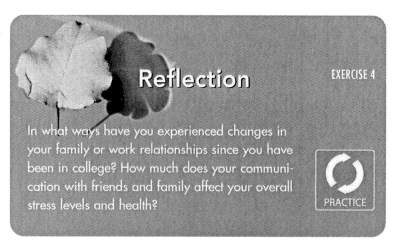

Reflection

EXERCISE 4

In what ways have you experienced changes in your family or work relationships since you have been in college? How much does your communication with friends and family affect your overall stress levels and health?

PRACTICE

Living a Balanced Life

Living a balanced life means paying attention to and improving all areas of your life—from relationships to cardiovascular health to your inner peace. If one area is overdeveloped, then the other areas will suffer from the lack of balance. There will be times that you will need to put in more hours at work and school, throwing the balance off slightly, but be careful that you make some time for the other areas that have been neglected.

A great way to stay balanced is to strive to create relationships with people on campus. Having healthy relationships with professors, advisors, and classmates will not only enable you to stay connected with your college work, but it will also provide you a personal support network in case you feel as though you need help with the stresses of being in college.

Balancing your life to eliminate stress also entails evaluating your values and priorities whenever you begin to feel stressed. You can then identify areas in your life that are getting out of balance and put those areas higher up on your list of priorities. For example, if you value exercise and are stressed because you realize that you have been spending most of your time at work or at school, you can make working out a higher priority, creating better balance in your life.

Getting Help When You Need It

An important part of making good choices and staying healthy is to get regular checkups and to see a health professional whenever you experience pain, difficulty, or even uncertainty about a health issue. Your college may provide access to a health clinic or health fairs. Free screenings, health seminars, and dispensing of over-the-counter medications are possible services that your college clinic may offer. Take advantage of these types of services, such as blood pressure checks or information about handling diabetes, because they may provide you with life-improving or life-saving information. If your college provides only limited access to health services, then you will need to find other ways to monitor your health. Regular checkups are part of taking care of yourself both in the short term and the long term.

Part of staying healthy is staying informed about health issues. Use what you have learned about finding reliable sources and determining their credibility when searching for information about your physical, mental, and psychological health.

BananaStock

Having healthy relationships provides a personal support network for you should you need help.

Never use information from the Internet to diagnose and treat yourself. Instead, if you find information that seems to pertain to your health issue, consider making an appointment with a doctor and provide him or her with your findings. Your doctor or health professional can help determine what the best course of action will be for you.

PLUS

EXERCISE 5

(Personality + Learning Style = Understanding Situations)

Let's revisit Evan's situation. He is a kinesthetic learner and extroverted; getting regular exercise and working out with others helps him stay healthy and release stress. However, his dedication to this sport has been taking away time and energy from college, and his coach doesn't seem very supportive of his competing activities. What advice can you give him that would help him be successful in college? Can he devote enough time to both parts of his life and expect to do well?

Now, considering your own learning style, personality type, and special circumstances, what would you do to stay focused on college when you find yourself challenged by competing priorities?

PROFILE

MY STORY
Learning Plan

Directions: Using what you have learned in this chapter and what you know about your learning preferences, choose a task or assignment that needs to be completed soon and create a learning plan that will help you accomplish this task. Then, write your *My Story* Summary, a one-sentence synopsis that crystallizes your newly created plan.

| LEARNING | |
| TASK | |

Time of Day

Intake Preference

Social Preference

Task Management Preference

MY STORY SUMMARY:

Path of Discovery

What are your top five health and stress issues?
What strategies will you use to address them?

HOMEWORK

From College to University

*How Your Stress Will Change and How to Handle
the New Pressures*

There are many possible stressors awaiting you when you make that move from your community college to university. Increased tuition, higher expectations, more difficult workload, impending graduation, and goal realization are all reasons to feel anxious about the transition, but remember that you have already succeeded in college by getting this far.

To meet the challenges that await you, be honest about them. For example, your professors will be asking more from you academically. In addition, recognize the fact that you will be graduating in just a few semesters and that you should plan for life after school. These realities, while daunting, do not have to be defeating if you are honest about them. With some work—and the good habits you form at your community college—you can overcome them with the same success.

Regardless of the new challenges, once you transfer, it will be even more important to have a solid support structure at work and at home. In addition, you will be making connections with people whom you hope will help you get a job after college. All of these relationships can provide you with a system for handling the demands of a four-year university. You will also need to be mindful of the stress-reducing strategies that work best for you. Practice them regularly and seek assistance in achieving your goals; you will then be more relaxed and more confident in your abilities.

From College to Career

Making Health Lifestyle Changes Is a Good Long-Term Strategy

Making healthy choices in college certainly has short-term results in that you will feel better and handle the negative effects of stress more effectively. However, the purpose of making better choices should be a long-term strategy to create a better life for you and your family. Therefore, when you complete your certificate or degree and enter into or back into the workforce, you may need to revise or reinforce your health goals. For example, you may have had time after classes to work out or play a sport as part of your exercise routine, but after graduation, you may have to change the time or place that you work out.

In addition to finding time to continue your positive health choices from college, you may also need to consider making your mental health part of your overall health plan. Maintaining healthy relationships with those who have positive influences on your life is one way to keep stress levels at a minimum and to create a safety net of friends and family when you may need them. Avoiding drugs, alcohol, and other poor health choices will be crucial to performing your best on the job. Some employers have strict policies about the use of drugs and alcohol on or off the job.

Because of the importance of good health, some employers have made keeping their employees healthy a top priority—it saves time and money in the long run when employees do not miss work because of illnesses. Talk with the human resources department about what your company offers its employees to support healthy habits. They may offer free screening, free or reduced-cost vaccinations, time off for doctors' appointments, health insurance, discounted gym memberships, and planned physical activities such as softball or basketball games.

Chapter Review Questions

1. What are the different ways students can incorporate exercise into their busy schedules?
2. What are the major health issues that college students face?
3. What can students do if they find themselves in an unhealthy relationship?
4. Predict what the effects will be for a student who makes poor health choices during a semester.
5. According to the categories listed in the chapter, evaluate how well you are improving or maintaining healthy habits.

Case Scenarios

1. Vin-Singh has been having trouble sleeping since he started college. He shares an apartment with another student who likes to stay up late and play loud music. Vin-Singh eats well and avoids caffeinated drinks, but he does not exercise regularly and often feels anxious when he tries to sleep. What advice can you give him for improving his sleep?

2. Wanda has not exercised since she was in high school, and now, 20 years later, she sees the importance of improving her health. In fact, she wonders if the 30 pounds she has gained since high school is keeping her from feeling her best when she juggles the demands of college. She is about to start her last year in college, one that will be stressful for her as she takes classes that will help her pass a licensing exam and get a good job. She also wants to lose the weight and start an aggressive exercise program. In light of what she is about to face, what advice can you give her?

3. Ever since D. J. started college, he has focused on his studies and has cut out all activities that do not help him achieve his educational goals. He has told his friends that he won't be able to hang out with them; he has cut back on his hours at work; he has stopped playing basketball and running; he has even stopped attending religious services so that he can have time to take as many class hours as possible each semester. He wants to graduate with a degree as fast as he can and start working, and his grades are good. However, after a few semesters, he has felt depressed and isolated, but he is not sure why. What advice can you give him?

Research It Further

1. Interview three people about their health habits. Find out what they do to maintain good health. Write down your findings and present them to your class.

2. Search the Internet for national statistics regarding violence against college students. Determine what groups are more likely to experience physical and sexual abuse. Inform your class of your findings.

3. What does your college offer in terms of health care for its students? Create a list of services and events along with contact numbers for community services that students may need. Present your list to your classmates.

References

American Heart Association. (2008). Cigarette smoking statistics. Retrieved May 16, 2008, from http://www.americanheart.org/presenter.jhtml?identifier=4559

Facts on Tap. Alcohol and student life. Retrieved May 16, 2008, from http://www.factsontap.org/factsontap/alcohol_and_student_life/index.htm

Gately, G. (2003, August 23). College students ignoring risks of unprotected sex. *Health Day News*. Retrieved August 29, 2005, from http://www.hon.ch/News/HSN/514968.html

Schoenherr, N. (2004). Depression, suicide are the major health issues facing college students, says student health director. *News & Information*. Washington University–St. Louis. Retrieved May 16, 2008, from http://news-info.wustl.edu/tips/page/normal/4198.html

U.S. Food and Drug Administration. (2004). How to understand and use the nutrition facts label. Retrieved May 16, 2008, from http://www.cfsan.fda.gov/~dms/foodlab.html

Glossary

Academic calendar—A list of important dates. Included are vacation breaks, registration periods, and deadlines for certain forms.

Academic probation—A student whose GPA falls below a designated number can be placed on academic probation. If the GPA does not improve, then the student may be prohibited from registering for classes for a designated number of semesters.

Articulation agreement—A signed document stating that one college will accept the courses from another college.

Associate of Applied Science—A degree that consists of about 60 credit hours of courses. Not intended to serve as a transferable degree to a four-year university.

Associate of Arts—A degree that consists of about 60 credit hours of general education courses. Often considered as the equivalent of the first two years of a four-year degree.

Audience—In essay writing, the audience is the person or persons whom you are addressing.

Catalog—A book that provides students with information about the college's academic calendar, tuition and fees, and degree/certificate programs.

Corequisite—A course that you can take at the same time as another course. For example, if intermediate algebra is a corequisite for physical science, then you will take both courses during the same semester.

Cornell System—A note-taking system in which a student draws an upside-down "T" on a sheet of paper and uses the space to the right for taking notes, the space to the left for adding questions and highlighting important points, and the space at the bottom for summarizing the material.

Course objective—A goal that the instructor has identified for the student to meet once the course is completed. For example, a course objective could be to use MLA documentation properly.

Cover letter—A letter accompanying a résumé that describes how a person's qualifications match the advertised requirements for the job.

Creative thinking—Thinking that creates or generates ideas.

Critical thinking—The ability to use specific criteria to evaluate reasoning and make a decision.

Curriculum—A term used to refer to the courses that a student must take in a particular field, or it can refer to all the classes that the college offers.

Developmental classes—Sometimes referred to as remedial classes, developmental classes focus on basic college-level skills such as reading, writing, and math. Students who earn a certain score on standardized tests such as the ACT and COMPASS exams may be required to take developmental classes before enrolling in college-level courses.

Family Educational Rights and Privacy Act (FERPA)—A federal law that ensures that a student's educational records, including test grades and transcripts, are not accessed or viewed by anyone who is not authorized by you to do so.

Full-time student—A student who is taking at least 12 credit hours of courses per semester.

Full-time worker—A person who is working at least 40 hours per week.

Grade point average (GPA)—The number that is used to determine a student's progress in college. It refers to the number of quality points divided by the number of hours a student has taken.

Knowledge—This comes from taking in information, thinking about it critically, and synthesizing one's own ideas about what one has read or seen.

Long-term goal—A goal that takes a long time to complete (within a year or more).

Major—The area that a student is focusing on for his or her degree. If a student wants to teach third grade, for example, his or her major can be elementary education. (*See also* Minor.)

Matching question—A test question that provides one column of descriptors and another column of words that must be matched with the appropriate descriptor.

Minor—A second area that a student can emphasize in his or her degree. A minor usually requires fewer classes and is not as intensive as a major. For example, if a student majors in marketing but also wants to learn more about running his or her own business, the student may want to minor in business or accounting.

Mission statement—A declaration of what a person or an institution believes in and what that person or institution hopes to accomplish.

Multiple-choice question—A type of test question in which an incomplete sentence or a question is given and the correct response must be chosen from a list of possibilities.

Objective question—A question that presents a limited number of possible answers.

OK5R—A reading strategy developed by Dr. Walter Pauk: overview, key ideas, read, record, recite, review, and reflect.

Part-time student—A student who is taking less than 12 credit hours per semester.

Prerequisite—A required course or score that must be completed or achieved before enrolling in a course.

Priority—Something that is important at that moment.

Purpose—What a student hopes to accomplish with his or her writing assignment.

Quality points—The number that is assigned to each grade. For example, an A is worth four quality points and a B is worth three quality points.

Remedial classes—*See* Developmental classes.

Résumé—A page or two that provides a person's educational and work experience, career objective, and contact information.

Short-term goal—A goal that can be accomplished in a short period of time (within a week or a few months).

SQ3R—A reading method that consists of the following elements: survey, question, read, recite, and review.

Stress—A physical and psychological response to outside stimuli.

Student handbook—A publication of the college that outlines what the college expects of the student.

Subjective question—A test question that requires a student to provide a personal answer. Usually, there are no "wrong" answers to subjective questions.

Syllabus—A document that contains an overview of the course, including objectives, assignments, and required materials as well as the instructor's policies for attendance, exams, and grading. It may also contain the college's policies on disability accommodations and academic dishonesty.

Time management—Strategies for using time effectively.

Topic—The subject of a piece of writing.

Transcript—A record of the courses a student has taken and the grades the student has earned. Transcripts also note the student's grade point average.

Transfer—Refers to moving from one school to another. Students who transfer must apply for admission to the second school and must request that their transcript(s) be sent to the new school.

T System—*See* Cornell System.

Values—Part of a person's belief system that provides the foundation of what the person does and what the person wants to become. If a person values financial stability, for example, then the person will look for opportunities to earn money and provide a secure future.

Work-study—A federal program that allows students to work at their college while taking classes. Students must qualify for work-study money and must meet college department requirements for work.

Appendix: VARK Learning Styles Inventory

There are a variety of ways to view yourself and how you learn. Although you are encouraged to explore your learning styles preferences and multiple intelligences, one inventory stands out for its ease of use and the empowerment students feel when they discover that they have a visual, aural, read/write, or kinesthetic learning preference or more than one.

Neil D. Fleming and Charles Bonwell have developed the VARK inventory, which uses the following categories for the learning styles preferences: Visual (V), Aural (A), Read/write (R), and Kinesthetic (K). If you have strong preferences in more than one mode, you are considered multimodal (MM).

VARK Inventory

Choose the answer which best explains your preference and circle the letter. Please select more than one response if a single answer does not match your perception.

Leave blank any question that does not apply.

1. You are helping someone who wants to go to your airport, town center or railway station. You would:
   a. go with her.
   b. tell her the directions.
   c. write down the directions.
   d. draw, or give her a map.

2. You are not sure whether a word should be spelled "dependent" or "dependant." You would:
   a. see the words in your mind and choose by the way they look.
   b. think about how each word sounds and choose one.
   c. find it in a dictionary.
   d. write both words on paper and choose one.

3. You are planning a holiday for a group. You want some feedback from them about the plan. You would:
   a. describe some of the highlights.
   b. use a map or website to show them the places.

    c. give them a copy of the printed itinerary.

    d. phone, text or email them.

4. You are going to cook something as a special treat for your family. You would:

    a. cook something you know without the need for instructions.

    b. ask friends for suggestions.

    c. look through the cookbook for ideas from the pictures.

    d. use a cookbook where you know there is a good recipe.

5. A group of tourists want to learn about the parks or wildlife reserves in your area. You would:

    a. talk about, or arrange a talk for them about parks or wildlife reserves.

    b. show them Internet pictures, photographs or picture books.

    c. take them to a park or wildlife reserve and walk with them.

    d. give them a book or pamphlets about the parks or wildlife reserves.

6. You are about to purchase a digital camera or mobile phone. Other than price, what would most influence your decision?

    a. Trying or testing it.

    b. Reading the details about its features.

    c. It is a modern design and looks good.

    d. The salesperson telling me about its features.

7. Remember a time when you learned how to do something new. Try to avoid choosing a physical skill, e.g., riding a bike. You learned best by:

    a. watching a demonstration.

    b. listening to somebody explaining it and asking questions.

    c. diagrams and charts—visual clues.

    d. written instructions—e.g., a manual or textbook.

8. You have a problem with your knee. You would prefer that the doctor:

    a. gave you a Web address or something to read about it.

    b. used a plastic model of a knee to show what was wrong.

    c. described what was wrong.

    d. showed you a diagram of what was wrong.

9. You want to learn a new program, skill or game on a computer. You would:

    a. read the written instructions that came with the program.

    b. talk with people who know about the program.

    c. use the controls or keyboard.

    d. follow the diagrams in the book that came with it.

10. You like websites that have:

    a. things you can click on, shift or try.

    b. interesting design and visual features.

    c. interesting written descriptions, lists and explanations.

    d. audio channels where you can hear music, radio programs or interviews.

11. Other than price, what would most influence your decision to buy a new nonfiction book?

    a. The way it looks is appealing.

    b. Quickly reading parts of it.

    c. A friend talks about it and recommends it.

    d. It has real-life stories, experiences and examples.

12. You are using a book, CD or website to learn how to take photos with your new digital camera. You would like to have:

    a. a chance to ask questions and talk about the camera and its features.

    b. clear written instructions with lists and bullet points about what to do.

    c. diagrams showing the camera and what each part does.

    d. many examples of good and poor photos and how to improve them.

13. Do you prefer a teacher or a presenter who uses:

    a. demonstrations, models, or practical sessions.

    b. question and answer, talk, group discussion, or guest speakers.

    c. handouts, books, or readings.

    d. diagrams, charts, or graphs.

14. You have finished a competition or test and would like some feedback. You would like to have feedback:

    a. using examples from what you have done.

    b. using a written description of your results.

    c. from somebody who talks it through with you.

    d. using graphs showing what you had achieved.

15. You are going to choose food at a restaurant or cafe. You would:

    a. choose something that you have had there before.

    b. listen to the waiter or ask friends to recommend choices.

    c. choose from the descriptions in the menu.

    d. look at what others are eating or look at pictures of each dish.

16. You have to make an important speech at a conference or special occasion. You would:

    a. make diagrams or get graphs to help explain things.

    b. write a few key words and practice saying your speech over and over.

    c. write out your speech and learn from reading it over several times.

    d. gather many examples and stories to make the talk real and practical.

Scoring. For each question, mark your answer below and then add up how many V's, A's, R's, and K's you have. The largest number of V, A, R, or K indicates your learning style preference. For example, if you marked "A" for question number 2, your learning style preference for that question is V. If you have more V's than any other letter, your learning style preference is Visual.

QUESTION	CHOICE A	CHOICE B	CHOICE C	CHOICE D
1	K	A	R	V
2	V	A	R	K
3	K	V	R	A
4	K	A	V	R
5	A	V	K	R
6	K	R	V	A
7	K	A	V	R
8	R	K	A	V
9	R	A	K	V
10	K	V	R	A
11	V	R	A	K
12	A	R	V	K
13	K	A	R	V
14	K	R	A	V
15	K	A	R	V
16	V	A	R	K

Calculating Your Score

Add the number of each letter and write the totals in the spaces below.

Total Number of V's circled _____

Total Number of A's circled _____

Total Number of R's circled _____

Total Number of K's circled _____

Look at your calculated score. If you have more V's than any other letter, then you have a strong visual learning preference. You may also have another learning style preference that is the same or close to your dominate learning style preference. For example, if you recorded 8 R's and 7 K's, you have both a read/write learning style preference as well as a kinesthetic learning style preference. Record your preference (s) in the space below.

My VARK Learning Style Preference is _____.

Index